HOUSES AND GARDENS OF
PORTUGAL

HOUSES AND GARDENS OF
PORTUGAL

MARCUS BINNEY AND PATRICK BOWE
NICOLAS SAPIEHA AND FRANCESCO VENTURI

CARTAGO

The author and photographers would like to thank the following
for their assistance: Maria Teresa Train; Dr Paulo Pereira;
Dr Inês Ferro; Marqueses Fernando and Amélia Albuquerque;
Counts of Vila Real; Fernando Mascarenhas, Marquis of
Fronteira; and the Foundation Casa de Fronteira e Alorno.
They would also like to thank the owners and curators of all the
other houses and gardens that appear in this book.

Published by CARTAGO, London
An imprint of KEA Publishing Services Ltd., 63 Edith Grove, London SW10 0LB

Copyright © KEA Publishing Services Ltd, London

Text © 1998 Marcus Binney and Patrick Bowe
Photographs © 1998 Nicolas Sapieha and Francesco Venturi except
Nicolas Sapieha/e.t.archive: 28–29; 57 top; 141; 152 left; 152 right; 153; 166–167; 168; 196; 210; 220–221.
Luis Pavão/Queluz: 30; 56–57; 58; 59 top; 59 bottom; 60–61.
Nuno Calvet/Fronteira Foundation: 43 top.
Sapieha/Fronteira Foundation: 43 bottom.
Venturi/Fronteira Foundation: 39.
Sapieha/Solar Mateus: 146; 164; 165 top; 165 bottom.

The Cataloguing in Publication data for this book is available from the British Library.

ISBN 1 900826 06 2

Designed by Karen Stafford
Edited by Anthony Lambert
Production by Elizabeth Harcourt
Picture Research by Maria Teresa Train
Map by Sarah-Jayne Stafford
Colour origination and printing by Amilcare Pizzi, Milan, Italy

www.keabooks.com

Jacket front

The unforgettable silhouette of the manor house of Mateus is doubled by
reflection in the still waters of a pool.

Jacket back

VILA VIÇOSA. The main corridor in the Paço dos Duques de Braganza.

Frontispiece

PAÇO DE VILA VIÇOSA. The re-created and carefully maintained box garden in
which Italian cypresses are used as striking focal points.

CONTENTS

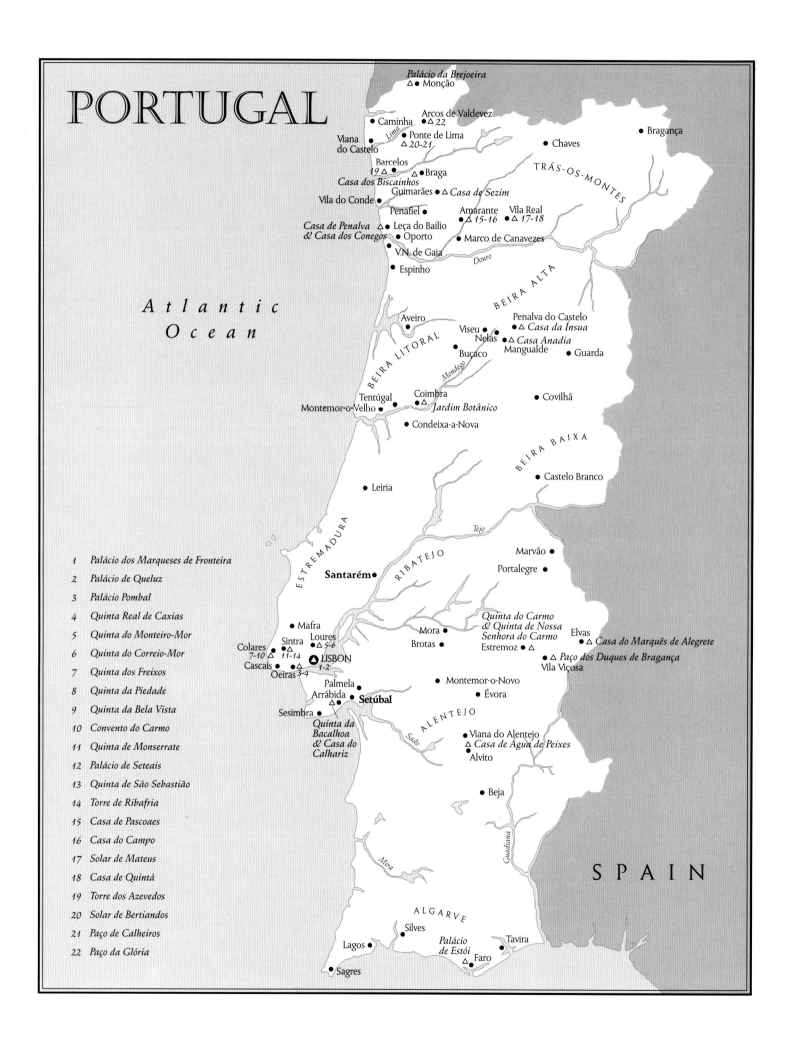

PORTUGAL

*Atlantic
Ocean*

Palácio da Brejoeira
△ ● Monção

● Caminha
Arcos de Valdevez
△ ● 22

Viana
do Castelo
● Ponte de Lima
△ 20-21

● Bragança

● Chaves

Barcelos
19 △ ●
△ ● Braga

Casa dos Biscainhos

TRÁS-OS-MONTES

Guimarães ● △ *Casa de Sezim*

Vila do Conde ●

Penafiel ●

Amarante
● △ 15-16

Vila Real
△ 17-18

Casa de Penalva
& Casa dos Conegos
△ ● Leça do Bailio
● Oporto

● Marco de Canavezes

V.N. de Gaia ●

Douro

BEIRA ALTA

● Espinho

Aveiro ●

Penalva do Castelo
● △ *Casa da Insua*

Viseu ●
Nelas ●
△ *Casa Anadia*
Mangualde

● Guarda

BEIRA LITORAL

Buçaco ●

Mondego

Tentúgal ●
Coimbra
●
△

Montemor-o-Velho ●

Jardim Botânico

● Covilhã

BEIRA BAIXA

● Condeixa-a-Nova

● Leiria

● Castelo Branco

Tejo

ESTREMADURA

RIBATEJO

● Marvão

Portalegre ●

Santarém ●

● Mafra

Loures
Sintra △ ● 5-6
Colares ● △
7-10 △ ● 11-14
Cascais ●
Oeiras 3-4 △ ●

LISBON
1-2

Mondego

Mora ●

Quinta do Carmo
& Quinta de Nossa
Senhora do Carmo

Elvas
● △ *Casa do Marquês de Alegrete*

Estremoz ● △

△ *Paço dos Duques de Bragança*
Vila Viçosa

Brotas ●

Palmela ●
Arrábida ●
Setúbal

Sesimbra ●

Quinta da
Bacalhoa
& Casa do
Calhariz

Sado

ALENTEJO

● Montemor-o-Novo

● Évora

● Viana do Alentejo
△ *Casa de Água de Peixes*
Alvito ●

● Beja

Guadiana

S P A I N

Mira

ALGARVE

● Silves

Palácio
de Estói
△ Faro

● Tavira

● Lagos

● Sagres

1   *Palácio dos Marqueses de Fronteira*
2   *Palácio de Queluz*
3   *Palácio Pombal*
4   *Quinta Real de Caxias*
5   *Quinta do Monteiro-Mor*
6   *Quinta do Correio-Mor*
7   *Quinta dos Freixos*
8   *Quinta da Piedade*
9   *Quinta da Bela Vista*
10   *Convento do Carmo*
11   *Quinta de Monserrate*
12   *Palácio de Seteais*
13   *Quinta de São Sebastião*
14   *Torre de Ribafria*
15   *Casa de Pascoaes*
16   *Casa do Campo*
17   *Solar de Mateus*
18   *Casa de Quintá*
19   *Torre dos Azevedos*
20   *Solar de Bertiandos*
21   *Paço de Calheiros*
22   *Paço da Glória*

INTRODUCTION

FOR CENTURIES THE MANOR HOUSE has been the principal focus of Portugal's rural life and work. Although it no longer dominates great landholdings as it did in the past, the manor house and its garden still form an integral part of Portugal's history. Frequently witness to great events, it is a potent physical symbol of the country's past, often saying more about it than any historical document. Many architectural histories prefer to measure a country's architectural progress in terms of its religious or civic buildings, but the most perceptive interpretations are derived from its domestic architecture which, after all, chronicles a way of life. The development of the manor house in Portugal is one of gradual evolution from an austere stone tower constructed for military defence to an exuberant elegant mansion designed to enhance the enjoyment of life.

Culturally Portugal seems to have been isolated from the rest of Europe at certain moments in its history, focusing more on its historic links with Africa, Asia and the Americas. These had been established before those of other European countries on account of Portugal's earlier seafaring prowess. This may explain how the early architectural and garden design movements current elsewhere in Europe came late to Portugal. It was not, for example, until the third decade of the sixteenth century that the Italian Renaissance style, already established in the fifteenth century, finally reached the Portuguese court and began to take the place of the medieval Gothic.

It is difficult to imagine that the squat, square medieval towers of simple stone construction, often located in remote upland, grassland or sea-girt locations, were the forerunners of the grand Portuguese manor house of later periods. They were not only its harbingers but for four centuries afterwards were often integrated into the later structures. Once powerful symbols of dominion over land and peasant, these towers remained, when incorporated in the new house, as symbols of a family's antiquity and heroic past.

One of the problems in discussing the Portuguese country house is what to call it. The term *solar*, evoking the light and elegance of a villa in the south, is used in the northern Minho region of the country. Further south and as far as the Tagus river, the term *quinta* is common. To complicate matters, the term *monte* is frequently used in the southern and eastern provinces of the Alentejo region. *Solar, quinta* and *monte*, like the better-known Italian word *villa*, are often used to designate not only the manor house itself but also the estate which surrounds it. The word *palácio* is reserved, as one might expect, for extra-large prodigy houses belonging to royalty and aristocracy alike. The term is often shortened in the north of Portugal to *paço*. To add further to a student's confusion, the simple word *casa*, meaning house, is sometimes used as the designation of an immense house of considerable architectural pretension. After the dissolution of the religious orders in Portugal in 1834, their monasteries and lands were purchased by members of the aristocracy and gentry who often retained in use the estate's original title of *convento* or *mosteiro*. Finally, when a manor house has been constructed around, or attached, to an earlier tower-house the word *torre* has been retained, often as the designation of the manor house as a whole.

The history of the villa and garden in Portugal begins with those of classical Rome, a glimpse of which we can still obtain today in the excavated city of Conimbriga near Coimbra.

Fortified tower-houses were a necessary response to the unsettled political situation which prevailed in medieval Portugal, not only as a result of the Moorish occupation from the eighth to the thirteenth centuries but also on account of continuing incursions from the neighbouring Iberian kingdoms, particularly Castile. The permanent installation of gardens was possible only within the precincts of the strongest castle or monastery and only on a small scale.

In the more settled fourteenth and fifteenth centuries, buildings of a more decorative nature in which the owner and his family might enjoy a greater degree of comfort were added to the earlier towers. A good example is the Solar de Pinheiros in the town

CASA DE ÁGUA DE PEIXES. Though the colonnade dates from different periods and is in different styles, unity is achieved through a harmonization of scale and materials.

of Barcelos; in the late fifteenth century, its two towers were linked by a residential wing of sober but elegant proportions and flanked by a courtyard. The towers' windows were enlarged, while decorative crenellations and gargoyles were added to the parapets.

The close of the Middle Ages and the beginning of the succeeding Renaissance period was a time of great change in Portugal. A country that once seemed remote and poor was entering an era of expansion and wealth due to the success of its mariners' explorations in distant parts of the world. This was accompanied by a period of great building characterized by a uniquely Portuguese style of late Gothic decoration known as Manueline, after King Manuel I (1495–1521). The style, which drew its exuberant inspiration from the epic voyages of the mariners, included, among a profusion of carved stone forms, depictions of the armillary sphere (the principal navigational aid of the time), twisted ropes, sails and exotic forms of vegetation discovered during the voyages, as well as depictions of The Cross of the Order of Christ, the pioneering Portuguese knightly order. In domestic architecture the Manueline style was particularly prevalent in the Alentejo province, where it was often combined in a curious way with Mudejar decoration (the Mudejar, or Moorish, style was then still prevalent in the south of Portugal as a result of the centuries of Moorish occupation). The principal manor houses in which the styles appear together are the sixteenth-century manor house of Paço de Sempre Noiva and Casa de Água de Peixes as well as in Paço de Giesteira, all in the Alentejo. The Manueline style expressed all the robust energy of a new age in Portugal. When it fell into decline around 1540, it was replaced by the new world and style of the Italian Renaissance.

The arrival of the Renaissance is evidenced in manor houses by the introduction of large, regularly spaced and often symmetrically arranged windows. This can be seen, for example, in the more domestic wing added to the late medieval tower-house of Torre de Ribafria near Sintra in 1534. However, the first more comprehensive adaptation of the Renaissance architectural and garden style can be seen in what must have been at the time (c.1480) a prodigy house, the Quinta da Bacalhoa. It was built for Braz de Albuquerque, a close friend of the royal princess, the Infanta Beatriz, near the village of Azeitão,

QUINTA DO CORREIO-
MOR. The 1744
church belfry acts as
a vertical focal point
for one of the
flanking box
parterres.

south of Lisbon. The design of Bacalhoa epitomizes a new openness to nature and the landscape around the house which was in marked contrast to the closed defensive character of the houses built before this period. Some of that new openness is illustrated in its two grand, first-floor colonnaded loggias overlooking the garden. But a more powerful illustration lies in the laying out of an extensive garden with pools and pavilions all designed as an integral part of the manor house's setting, the lines of the architecture being carefully projected out into the lines of the garden's design. Although Italian in its overall inspiration, one feature of the house and garden anticipates an important element of all subsequent Portuguese house and garden styles – the use of walls of decorative tiles, some of which derived from Moorish designs illustrating the continuity of artistic craftsmanship since the Moorish occupation of Portugal, while others are major examples of pictorial tilework which ultimately became the key component of the Portuguese decorative arts tradition.

Much of the seventeenth century was a period of economic hardship and bleak austerity in Portugal, a time of depression in marked contrast to what had preceded it and what was to follow. For almost 30 years, the country was at war with Spain, whose king, Philip II, was a nephew of Portugal's King João III and had seized the Portuguese crown in 1580. During the Spanish occupation of Portugal, Philip II constructed a palace and laid out a garden in Lisbon. However, during this time few major buildings or gardens were created. At the end of hostilities between the two countries, one grand manor house and garden were designed almost by way of celebration of Portugal's recovered independence. This was Palácio de Fronteira, begun in 1669 at the behest of the 1st Marquês de Fronteira, João de Mascarenhas, one of Portugal's great generals who had been instrumental in inflicting a major defeat on the Spanish forces.

Fronteira reflects in its concept and execution the Italian Renaissance ideal of a house and garden integrated in one overall design. However, here, as at Bacalhoa, that ideal is overlaid with the distinctive Portuguese tradition of using extensive glazed decorative tilework. Although at Fronteira the tiles are combined principally to depict solemn and monumental pictures of Portuguese kings as well as classical deities, it is the smaller polychromatic pictures illustrating picaresque, often humorous, subjects which can be marked out as truly Portuguese in spirit.

The eighteenth century was an important period in the history of Portuguese architecture and design. As a result of the great wealth accruing from its colonies, especially from the mining of gold and precious stones in the Minas Gerais and in the Serra of São Paolo, both in Brazil, austerity was replaced by exuberance in artistic language – the language of the Portuguese baroque which was named Joanine in honour of the king, João V, himself a great patron of the arts. Of all the architectural and garden styles which make up the Portuguese inheritance, this seems to today's visitor the most characteristic of all. There are many splendid examples of manor houses in this style in almost every region of Portugal. Exceptionally memorable are a number of prodigy houses in the north of the country which were erected to the designs of an inspired Italian architect, Nicolau Nasoni. Although the decoration of his houses is extraordinary, it was his innovations in the planning of both the exterior and interior of manor houses which was to have more lasting effect. At the Palácio do Freixo near Oporto and at the Solar de Mateus by Vila Real, he pioneered the use of a monumental external double staircase leading from the entry court-

PALÁCIO DE FRONTEIRA. 'Poetry', one of a set of tile-panels representing the Liberal Arts which are set into the wall of the Chapel Walk.

yard to the principal rooms of the house on the *piano nobile*, or the first floor, of raised formal terraces overlooking the garden, of façades advancing and receding in curving planes and of spectacular sculptural decoration which reached its most theatrical and fantastical in the centre block of the manor house at Mateus. The elaborate façades of Portugal's baroque country houses were often augmented by the incorporation in the design of a family chapel, which in former periods had stood separately in another part of the grounds. With the close of this great period of baroque architecture, the country house in Portugal had already reached its apogee.

A period of great complexity in architecture and garden design is often followed by a reaction in favour of a purer, simpler approach. At this time, the complex baroque and rococo styles were succeeded by the simpler Neo-classical style in which designers and their patrons returned for inspiration to the basic elements of classical Greek architecture and design. Although not many Portuguese manor houses and their gardens were created in this style, important examples survive. These include the impressive Palácio de Seteais near Sintra and the austere garden with its temple of the Casa do Calhariz located on the edge of the natural park of Arrábida, south of Lisbon.

SOLAR DE MATEUS. Elaborate baroque architectural detail builds up in a crescendo towards the centre of the house.

The study of Portuguese architecture and design during the eighteenth and nineteenth centuries also offers an excellent introduction to the principles of manor house design in places such as Madeira, the Azores, Brazil, Goa, Macau and also the former African colonies of Portugal. All of these places have excellent examples of historic domestic architecture to delight the present-day visitor. If the Portuguese manor house exported its traditions to these far-flung places, it also derived from them many of its architectural traditions as well as many of the plants used in its gardens. The upward tilt of the eaves of many houses in Portugal derives ultimately from China. Long, low, shady verandahs have their origin in the tropical climates of many former Portuguese colonies. The complex, eclectic house which was built in the late nineteenth century in an *art nouveau* or *fin de siècle* architectural style is often known as a *casa brasileira* or Brazilian house because it was generally built by a Portuguese retiring to his homeland after making a fortune in Brazil.

In order to study and propagate the growing influx of exotic plants from these colonized countries, botanical gardens were developed in Lisbon in 1772 and in Coimbra in 1774. Much later, in 1906, the Jardim Tropical was founded near Lisbon at Belém (where, appropriately enough, Vasco de Gama's tomb is located) with the task of making more specific scientific, botanical studies of plants from the colonies. The new range of plants becoming available could not be easily incorporated within the confines of the traditional manor house formal garden. So a new kind of expanded landscape garden, based on the naturalistic style of the English garden, was developed to deploy the newly imported plants to advantage. The perfect natural setting and climate for this new type of garden already existed at Sintra, a dramatic wooded ridge with a cool climate located north of Lisbon. There, a number of important gardens in this new style were made, including that of the royal summer palace of Pena, at the romantic Moorish-style house of Monserrate and at the neo-Manueline house of Quinta da Regaleira.

The development of steam technology allowed designers and their clients greater freedom of movement by rail and ship than ever before; as a result they came to experience a wider variety of geographical and historical architectural and garden styles than ever before. Craftsmen, their materials and products also enjoyed greater freedom of movement, as did gardeners, nurserymen and their plants. Thus the opportunity to create houses and gardens in new romantic and imaginative ways became more widely available, so that no one design style was dominant at this period – rather, a host of different styles.

Those who took this opportunity were not initially from the traditional class of Portuguese landowner but from a new group of patrons who were not tied by family or land to an old Portuguese manor house tradition. The first, and perhaps the most important, was the King-Consort Ferdinand II, husband of Queen Maria II. In his native Germany, the adaptation of historicist styles for use in contemporary buildings had been current since the beginning of the nineteenth century. It is not surprising therefore that when he came to build a new royal summer palace on a ridge overlooking Sintra, he would employ in its design a whole range of different historic architectural styles somehow welded together into a romantic, if eclectic, whole. On the slopes below the palace he laid out landscape gardens which were freely planted with exotic trees and shrubs. Most notable were two ravines planted with New Zealand tree ferns.

Overleaf

CASA DO CALHARIZ. The man-made precision of fountain and parterre are in dramatic contrast with the wildness of the landscape beyond.

The fresh colours of variegated ivy leaf and pelargonium flowers seen in counterpoint with the fading paint of the wall behind.

Opposite PALÁCIO DE FRONTEIRA. A typical palimpsest of tiles of different periods with granite balustrades and benches.

Two other significant houses and gardens at Sintra were made for millionaires: Quinta de Monserrate for the English textile magnate Sir Francis Cook and Quinta da Regaleira for Carvalho Monteiro who had made a fortune in Brazil. The latter was in the neo-Manueline style, considered the most patriotic of the styles available because it revived for contemporary usage a uniquely Portuguese late medieval architectural and decorative style. The neo-Manueline finally gained official acceptance as a manor house style in 1906 when King Carlos chose it for the new summer palace he planned for the ancient forest of Buçaco in central Portugal.

As in the case of the earlier Neo-classical reaction against the sometimes excessive decoration of the baroque, so in the early twentieth century a purifying reaction set in against the complex and varied *fin de siècle* eclectic styles. This reaction was to become known as the Modern or International Modern style. Portugal is lucky to have an outstandingly well-maintained house and garden in this austere style – the Casa de Serralves in Oporto.

An austere style also characterized much of Portugal's post-World War II buildings and their gardens. Good examples are the landscape gardens of the Gulbenkian Foundation (1969) in Lisbon and of the public gardens of Jardim do Entroncamento (1981) at Tomar and the Jardim Visconde de Luz (1984) at Cascais. A similarly modern school of landscape design developed in the province of the Algarve which aimed to integrate the leisure facilities required by tourists – golf courses, tennis courts, swimming-pools – into an overall landscape setting. The resort known as Quinta do Lago is an excellent example.

However, the private manor house and its garden continued throughout the twentieth century to be created predominantly in a number of different traditional styles. The gardens of the Quinta da Piedade at Sintra, the Quinta dos Girassóis at Maia, north of Oporto, and the Quinta do Vale at Loures, for example, have much architectural decoration and planting in traditional Portuguese style, yet they are compact in size and compartmentalized in layout, even if more diverse in their planting schemes than the traditional garden.

As the twentieth century nears its close, an attempt has been made to marry the modernist architectural style, with its advanced technology and new materials, and traditional architectural forms. The style resulting from this attempt has become known as Post-modernism. Portugal has a number of outstanding villas and gardens in this latest design style, especially in the region of the Algarve. So the tradition of the Portuguese manor house and its garden is not just an historic one but also one that is living today as we approach the twenty-first century.

LISBON AND THE TAGUS

WITHIN THE REGION OF LISBON, country manors have a distinctly urban character and are surrounded by luxurious gardens. The different architectural styles of the Renaissance, the baroque, the rococo and the Neo-classical are vividly expressed in façades, in the decoration of interiors and in gardens.

In 1521, Braz de Albuquerque, a natural son of Afonso de Albuquerque, the great mariner and soldier who conquered Goa, accompanied the Infanta Beatriz on a visit to Italy. He must have been impressed by the new architecture of the Italian Renaissance, its rational simplicity and restraint in total contrast to the exuberance and intricacy of the late Gothic architecture still dominant in Portugal. On his return to Lisbon, he began to build a town palace, the Casa dos Bicos, in which each stone of the façade is cut like a faceted diamond. (This was a device sometimes used in the design of Italian palaces, such as the Palazzo dei Diamanti in Ferrara.)

In 1528, Albuquerque acquired the Quinta da Bacalhoa which is located on the Arrábida peninsula south of Lisbon: the area had been popular as a royal hunting ground since the previous century. He began to construct a country villa on the model of those he had seen in Italy, with open-air loggias and gardens where not only luxurious living but also cultural humanist activities might be enjoyed and appreciated. To give an underlying unity of design, the whole estate, together with all its buildings, was laid out using the simple geometric formula of the square.

Over the entrance gate is inscribed the name of Albuquerque and the date 1554, perhaps the date the villa was completed. Upon passing through the gate, the visitor steps into a large square courtyard, its apparent size increased by its bareness. Two features immediately catch the eye: the corner towers with domes based on the form of the lotus flower (Albuquerque's connection with India has already been noted) and the enclos-

Previous page

QUINTA DA BACALHOA. A waterside loggia
in classical Renaissance style has a later
up-tilted roof.

ing early Renaissance-style arcades. The house itself lies across the courtyard to the left. Tall classically proportioned windows, capped by niches, reveal that the main apartments are on the second floor. A massive and imposing staircase leading up to them is unexpectedly asymmetrical, but this easily goes unnoticed amid the virtuoso display on its flanks of *azulejos* which are Moorish in character and among the earliest in Portugal.

After the large bare expanse of the courtyard, the garden on the other side of the house comes as an enchanting surprise; here all is lush, green and beautifully tended. The layout is seen to best advantage from the loggia on the second floor. A square box garden extends around a sparkling central fountain. Each quarter of the design is different. In one corner the word *Roi* traced in box can be seen. To one side, a high yew hedge which balances a projecting wing of the house also conceals a wall seat with a tiled back panel depicting the Rape of Europa, as described in Ovid's *Metamorphoses*.

Beyond and below the box garden lies a sunken tangerine grove. The domed canopies of its trees shade neat rows of silvery artichokes and bluish kale that contrast vividly with the reddish soil. To the side, a raised walk designed for evening promenading is lined with tiled seats and raised flower-boxes which are now filled with climbing roses, geraniums, stonecrops, lavenders and helichrysums. The boxes are faced with glazed tiles which reflect rather than absorb heat and so protect the roots of the plants within from drying out in summertime.

The third section of the garden comprises a large water tank or pool flanked on one side by an elegant arcaded pavilion. The raised tank is kept unusually full, bringing the water closer to the visitor's eye-level. In his book *The Education of a Gardener* (1962), Russell Page remarks that as a result of this device 'light shimmers off the water and the reflected trees and hills are more strangely diffused because of the unusually low angle of vision'.

Inside the waterside pavilion, the walls are covered with large green and yellow tiles in traditional Moorish patterns. There is one figurative panel, depicting the biblical story of Susannah and the Elders and which carries the date 1565. When W.C. Watson, author of *Portuguese Architecture* (1908), visited, he saw della Robbia-style medallions but these have since disappeared. A raised promenade continues around the pool and along the estate wall past the elegant parish church to a summer-house known as the Casa da India, so called because it originally contained paintings of the Indian cities subdued by Afonso de Albuquerque at the beginning of the sixteenth century. The comprehensiveness of the estate's original design is further illustrated in the dovecote and six boundary towers, all boasting ribbed domes to match those of the house.

Albuquerque, the creator of the estate, died without children in 1581 and, for a period of about three centuries, Bacalhoa was owned by a succession of owners, none of whom carried out any major alterations. In 1890, it was inherited by the 2nd Conde de Mesquitella. A set of watercolours executed by an artist called Blanc in 1898 show a house still of pure Renaissance character. However, soon after the declaration of the republic in 1910, the estate was sold. Photographs taken thirty years later show the house in pitiful condition. The arcade in the courtyard has collapsed, the roof of the north wing has fallen in, and the loggia overlooking the parterre lies in pieces on the floor, though the tiles around the walls remain unscathed. But by this time, in 1937, a saviour had discovered Bacalhoa – Mrs Herbert Scoville, an American lady of quite exceptional taste and sensitivity.

Her reconstruction is a model of its kind; she used the evidence of Blanc's water-colours to restore the house exactly to its former state. Inside, much of the decorative detail has been lost, but she relaid floors in characteristic brick tile and remade the great wooden trapezoidal ceilings using Finnish pine, apparently much in vogue in Portugal at that time. Plain whitewashed walls emphasize the noble proportions of the rooms, and elegant, low sofas and armchairs are set off by occasional dark, handsome, early chests and cupboards.

The most important survival is the set of tile panels portraying river gods in the loggia. These have strapwork frames clearly inspired by Flemish mannerism: the great authority Santos Simões has identified them as the work of Marcelo de Matos, a Portuguese pupil of the Flemish ceramic artist Philippe de Goes. The house also contains two small but interesting staircases. The first is an unusual double stair in the north-east tower; its matching flights descend precipitously on either side of a massive central newel. The second descends to a pretty room with an elaborate ceiling, perhaps dating from the eighteenth century. Here the central newel is hollowed out to form a snake-like handrail.

Mrs Scoville's judicious modern planting enlivens the existing garden structure. Banksian roses, dark purple bougainvilleas and the climbing aloe, *Aloe arborescens*, now scale the walls; succulent euphorbias, spreading helichrysum and hanging ballota fill the raised beds. Freesias scent the parterres in spring and belladonna lilies flower under clipped hibiscus during the summer. Stately arum lilies contrast with the drooping bells of the rare *Buddleja colvilei* and a walk lined with succulent aeoniums is enclosed by hedges of bridal wreath. 'For sheer boldness and simplicity of plan', wrote Russell Page in his article 'Some Portuguese Gardens' (1935), 'the garden is one of the most striking in all of European art.'

Near Bacalhoa is another Renaissance house and garden of the first rank, the Quinta das Torres. Built around a courtyard and with high pyramidal roofs and a Palladian portico, it boasts a raised water tank with an open, domed pavilion standing in the middle. Similarly located pavilions are known also from records of Moorish gardens in Sicily and Spain and of Moghul gardens in India.

FRONTEIRA

The English traveller William Hickey, who was in Portugal in 1782, says his host entertained at Benfica near Lisbon 'in a manner never surpassed and seldom equalled... The establishment was in every respect princely, the house a perfect cabinet, the grounds laid out with peculiar taste, having in them all the rarest plants of the European world and some even from Asia and America but what delighted me most was the songs of the nightingales innumerable pouring out their sweet notes in broad daylight.'

The quinta at Benfica belonged to Gerard de Visme and Marianne, daughter of the Marquis of Magans, French Huguenots who had fled as refugees to England and subsequently set up in business in Portugal. In 1836, Lord Carnarvon described Benfica in glowing terms as 'a place greatly resorted to by the Portuguese nobles, and surrounded with orange groves and cork woods; and well indeed their deep green colour contrasted with the dazzling whiteness of the villas and quintas which adorn this beautiful valley.'

The finest of these *quintas* today is undoubtedly the Palace of the Marquesses of Fronteira. It is displayed full frontal to the road, clearly visible through a tall but airy wrought-iron screen. Statues of a warrior and a beauty stand on the gate-piers. The house behind immediately proclaims the Renaissance love of the open air, with a double loggia filling the whole centre of the façade. Pairs of columns – the sturdy Doric below, the slender Ionic above – alternate with arches.

The house can be dated quite precisely from contemporary descriptions. One visitor was the Marchese Corsini who came with Cosimo de Medici on 7 February 1669. He observed: 'The dwelling is presently under construction, is being built with economy and taste and has a garden adjacent to it with diverse parterres, statues and *bas reliefs*. There are five great fountains and others, smaller but of differing heights, on differing levels in the garden... so far the Marquess has spent over 50,000 cruzados and there is still much left to do.' The palace was built for João de Mascarenhas who was created Marquess of Fronteira in 1670. He was a close confidant of the Regent, Pedro, who seized power from his brother, King Afonso VI, at the end of the War of Restoration in 1667.

Fronteira has a formal garden as perfect and memorable as any in Europe. It is in the form of a vast box parterre quartered and further quartered around a set of five fountains to make sixteen separate sections in all. The Great Fountain at the centre celebrates in stone the builder's family; the Mascarenhas coat of arms is held aloft above a representation of an armillary sphere – a celestial globe comprising rings representing the equator, the tropics and so on, which has often been used by Portuguese sculptors to commemorate their country's maritime achievements. Beneath the sphere, water spills from four shell-like basins, splashing over four piping cherubs before falling into a large circular basin with four angular projections corresponding to the garden's axes.

At first, symmetry appears to prevail. However, a closer examination of the parterre and its interlocking patterns of squares, circles and diamonds reveals that one half of the parterre is larger than the other and that the box pattern in each of its quarters is different in detail from the others. Stone figures standing on curiously outsized pedestals post-date the box parterre and include copies of famous originals such as the Venus de Medici and the Dancing Faun. The entire garden is surrounded by a low wall with recessed

Opposite PALÁCIO DE FRONTEIRA. Lichen colours the mannerist-style balustrade of the great tank. In the background, a figure of Mercury tops the pyramidal-roofed pavilion of the Gallery of Kings.

PALÁCIO DE FRONTEIRA. An oblique view from
the first-floor gallery showing the
relationship between the box parterre. the
great tank and the King's Gallery above.

seats and *alegretes* – built-in, raised flower-boxes characteristic of the Portuguese garden – all covered with blue-and-white tile pictures depicting a medley of picaresque, genre and allegorical scenes.

Tanks, usually placed at the highest part of the garden, were a necessary feature of the old gardens of Portugal to provide water for the house and garden during summer droughts. The Great Tank at Fronteira is unusually sited, since it adjoins the low-level parterre and is designed integrally with it. Flower vases soften the line of its surrounding balustrade, and four diminutive stone figures are placed so as to appear standing on its water. A wall, 15 feet high and divided into fifteen arches, rises at the back of the tank. Twelve of the arches are blind and filled with tile-pictures depicting knights on prancing chargers in the manner of Velasquez's equestrian portraits. The remaining three arches open into grottos, the middle one containing a copy of the Pegasus fountain at the Villa Aldobrandini at Frascati near Rome. This may have been copied from Falda's engraving of the Villa Aldobrandini published in 1675. All of the arches are outlined with life-like garlands of fruit and foliage and rest on columns entwined with simulated laurel leaves; their spandrels are encrusted with pebbles and their friezes with shells. The richness of decoration becomes almost a surfeit through its reflection in the tank's water.

Great staircases rise by the tank's sides to pyramid-roofed pavilions which are topped by copies of Giambologna's *Mercury* serving as finials. Between the pavilions stretches a high balustraded terrace, the centre of which is marked by an open stone portal that neatly frames a view of the house and garden behind. At the back of the terrace is a high wall punctuated with niches corresponding to the arches of the tank below. Each niche, outlined by ceramic pineapples with a copper-coloured lustre glaze, contains a bust of one of the Portuguese kings – hence the terrace's name of Kings' Promenade.

While the house, parterre, tank and terrace can be viewed together in one glance, the rest of the garden gradually unfolds in a series of carefully calculated surprises. The first, known as the Star Garden after its central star-shaped pool, has evolved from a nineteenth-century garden of winding paths and naturalistic plantings. The chief survivor of the latter among the present arrangement of formal beds is a monumental bunya-bunya pine, *Araucaria bidwillii*, a native of Queensland, Australia, which towers over the palace.

The Sunken Garden is centred on a pool edged with stone scrolls and fountains in the manner of the pool of the Khas Mahal in the fort of Agra in India. Behind is a grotto with a façade based on a published drawing of the Italian sixteenth-century architect Vignola. Inside and out, the grotto is thickly encrusted with shell and pebble decoration for which, in a delightful whimsy, whole china plates are also pressed into service. The garden is surrounded by a continuous built-in seat faced with allegorical and genre tile-pictures in a *faux-naif* style, some of comic-strip hilarity.

The Chapel Promenade displays an exceptional example of Renaissance-style Portuguese garden architecture. Its backing wall is divided into a blind arcade with arches containing tile-pictures of the muses alternating with niches containing stone figures of the gods from the Orphic mysteries. Above the niches are della Robbia-style medallions which must be those referred to by the Marchese Corsini in 1699.

A Renaissance garden was designed for the enjoyment of the arts as well as luxurious living. Therefore, the garden at Fronteira must have enjoyed a special flowering during the early nineteenth century when it was inhabited by Leonor d'Almeida, 4th Marchioness of Alorna. Her salon was among the most frequented in Europe according to the French minister to Portugal, the Count of Saint Priest. Under the pen name Alcipe, she wrote poems including one celebrating the enjoyment of botany as a recreation. The present Marquês and Marchioness of Fronteira and Alorna have established a foundation to ensure the future of the house and garden, which are among the most important in Portugal.

The name of Pombal dominates a whole era of Portuguese history in the same way that the name of Richelieu does in France or Bismarck in Germany. As the visitor approaches the Palácio de Pombal, expectations are aroused of a palace on a colossal scale; the best intimation is the massive octagonal dovecote on a lonely hillside which contains over a thousand nesting boxes.

The palace stands in the bustling little town of Oeiras. Pombal inherited the property in 1737 and probably began building immediately. His architect was Carlos Mardel, best known for his work on the Aguas Livres, the great aqueduct that brings water to Lisbon. The entrance front, preceded by a formal *cour d'honneur*, is decidedly French, but on the garden front architectural details appear which are clearly taken from the work of the Roman architect Borromini. His book of engravings, *Opera*, published in 1720, is the major source of the more exotic and bizarre decorative detail in mid-eighteenth-century Portuguese architecture. Two signatures of the Borromini style are tweaked pediments and false perspective. Both are used in the design of the palace at Pombal, the latter over the ground-floor windows where stone scrolls are angled so as to suggest to the viewer that they are in higher relief than they are in reality.

The palace today is in immaculate condition, but is in institutional use and not open to the public. However, there is admission to the gardens which contain two most unusual features. The first is a grotto dramatically encrusted with rough rockwork and studded with cave-like arches. From a high level, water drips from one encrusted bowl to the next, creating pockets of moisture in which mosses and ferns flourish around the figure of a reclining river god which forms the focus of the whole composition. Its roof, decorated with balustrades and deliberately oversized busts, acts as a vantage point for viewing the garden. The garden's second unusual feature is a double staircase clad with tile-pictures framed in rococo cartouches. The scenes portray the stories of Mars and Venus and of Perseus and Andromeda. Inside the staircase, the central vault is clad with a composition created with fragments of broken porcelain; as well as the usual Chinese blue-and-white china, fragments and whole plates of *famille rose* add rich accents of red. The broken porcelain, intermingled with seashells and semi-precious stones, gleams in the vault's half-light.

After the disastrous earthquake that hit Lisbon in 1755, the king's eldest son, later to reign as José I, built a new palace on the hill of Ajuda, some miles west of Lisbon and out of the earthquake zone. In front of the palace, he constructed a magnificent balustraded terrace garden overlooking the River Tagus. Of the balustrade William Beckford wrote, 'I never saw a balustrade better hewn or chiselled'. The lower terrace was planted as a shady woodland garden. Beckford remarked on its air of coolness provided by three fountains and augmented 'by the waiving [sic] of planes and acacias'.

Dom José established a royal botanic garden at Ajuda in 1768. Its first director, an Italian botanist, Domenico Vandelli, was succeeded by another Italian, Giulio Mazziatti. But when the new palace burned down in 1794 and its replacement was built on the hill above, the garden was left isolated. In 1807, Laura Junot, wife of Napoleon's ambassador to Portugal, noted that it had been overtaken in importance by the botanic garden in Coimbra. It enjoyed a brief revival under the directorship of Felix de Avelar Brotero between 1811 and 1828. One of the more renowned botanists in Portuguese history, Brotero catalogued no fewer than 1,200 species growing there. Many were from Angola, Brazil and the Cape Verde Islands, all Portuguese colonies. A second brief revival of the Ajuda garden's fortunes occurred between 1840 and 1844 under the directorship of Frederic Welwitsch, an Austrian medical doctor and amateur botanist. Now no more than a public park, it is still used, however, by the Institute of Agronomy for the teaching of gardening.

Vestiges of the garden's former glory both as a botanic and a royal garden remain. Today, a vast parterre in an unexpectedly twentieth-century Art Deco style surrounds a magnificent original fountain, appropriately awash with sculpted figures of sea creatures.

PALÁCIO DE POMBAL. A white marble figure on the garden balustrade.

The balustrades mentioned by Beckford, together with fine flights of steps, niches and glazed pots delightfully stamped with the royal cipher, survive. Some superb trees, including a dragon tree, 20 feet high and 50 feet across, remain. (Other major specimens of this tree can be enjoyed in the park of the Palacio das Necessidades and in the Lisbon University Botanic Gardens.) An Australian silk oak, *Grevillea robusta,* is particularly spectacular when it opens its golden-yellow flowers in spring; a South African tree fuchsia, *Schotia latifolia,* is covered with red, fuchsia-like flowers at the same season. These and a large kangaroo thorn, *Acacia armata,* are living representations of the cosmopolitan collection of trees that once grew there.

The greatest combinations of house and garden are those in which landscape and architecture balance and reflect each other to such a degree that one seems inconceivable without the other. Queluz, a royal summer palace in the hills outside Lisbon, is one of the few places where this elusive unity has been achieved. Built by a team of architects and sculptors over a period of sixty years, Queluz betrays few of the incongruous lapses of design that so often hamper projects directed by more than one person.

The transformation of the old manor house which existed on the site into a palace was begun in 1747 at the order of the future King Pedro III under the direction of the Portuguese architect Mateus Vicente (1747–86). About ten years later, Jean-Baptiste Robillion (d. 1782), who was a follower of Thomas Germain, the Parisian goldsmith much patronized by the Portuguese court, was introduced to the future King Pedro. He took over the building project at Queluz, developing it along the lines of Louis XIV's woodland retreat known as Marly, which is also U-shaped, encloses sunken gardens and is deliberately modest in proportions.

The palace reception rooms open directly on to a terrace surrounding a sunken box parterre. The parterre is notable for its two principal fountains whose asymmetrically composed sculptural groups are in the rococo style. Both fountains illustrate stories from the Greek mythology of the sea god Poseidon. The first fountain, usually known as the Fountain of Neptune, is a representation of the mythic contest that took place between Poseidon and Athena to see which of them could offer the greater gift to mankind. Poseidon is depicted striking a rock from which emerges Pegasus, the world's first horse. Athena is depicted planting, as her gift to mankind, an olive tree in the cleft of the rock from which Pegasus is seen to emerge. Although the outcome of the contest is not depicted in the fountain, the fact that Athena's olive branch was declared the winner must have made the myth seem an appropriate one for a garden fountain.

The second of the principal fountains, called the Fountain of the Nereid, represents the sea nymph Thetis with whom Poseidon fell in love. The fountain's sculptor has shown her at the moment in the myth when she rises from the waves, bearing aloft on trays the jewels made for her in her undersea cavern by the god of metalworking, Hephæstus. The theme of Poseidon and Athena is continued in the sculptural pieces decorating the gate-piers at the exit from the parterre. These are depictions of Pegasus after his capture by Bellerophon (which became possible only after Athena had provided him with a bridle).

In gardens like Queluz, overall consistency of sculptural theme is rare. Thus, in addition to the Poseidon- and Athena-related figures, the garden contains a motley collection of statues on other themes: some figures are depicted in medieval armour; others

are in eighteenth-century costumes; and some are of monkeys or dolphins. Others are allegorical figures representing the Four Seasons. There is even a copy of Giambologna's *Samson and the Philistines* which is recorded as having been ordered from John Cheere's workshop in London. Of all this subsidiary statuary, the most memorable is a pair of stone sphinxes with women's heads and lions' bodies which are dressed in fashionable eighteenth-century masquerade costume.

PALÁCIO DE QUELUZ. The fountain of the sea nymph Thetis, who rose from the sea on the back of a dolphin bearing aloft the trays of jewels made for her by the sea-god Hephæstus.

PALÁCIO DE QUELUZ. The small salon or sitting-room of Dona Maria Francisca Benedita, Princess of Brazil (1746-1829), is decorated in a light, Neo-classical style using mirrored doors and *trompe-l'oeil* in the shallow domed ceiling. The room is furnished with painted chairs featuring feathered and garlanded backs.

The adjoining formal garden was originally intended for the reception of ambassadors. It has always been called the Garden of Malta because its original box pattern is said to have been based on the Maltese Cross. Topiary, not statuary, dominates this garden which is ringed by a terrace, the steps to which weave in and out in a manner described by Russell Page as being that of 'a writing master's arabesques'. Stone balustrades capped with urns and statues surround both these gardens and divide them from the woodland garden beyond. Radiating outwards from the Pegasus Gate, a series of carriage drives leads through the woodland to the garden's boundaries. The first ends at an artificial water cascade completed in 1780. A second leads to the Lisbon Gate while a third leads down a hill to the confluence of the garden's two boundary streams. The areas between the drives were originally thickly planted with lime and elm trees. Records indicate that in 1751 alone, 800 limes and 240 elms were imported from Holland for planting in this area. Most of these trees had died by 1935 when Russell Page reported the wood as being composed of eucalyptus trees. Today the area is scattered with a mixture of trees, but it is hoped that the original planting of elms and limes will be reinstated.

William Beckford (1760–1844), the English writer and collector, stopped at the gardens of Queluz one evening after a visit to the monastery of Alcobaça. There he met the Infanta, the daughter-in-law of the king. He later wrote of the encounter as follows:

> Cascades and fountains were in full play: a thousand sportive *jets d'eau* were sprinkling the rich masses of bay and citron, and drawing forth all their odours, as well-taught water is certain to do on all such occasions. Among

the thickets, some of which received a tender light from tapers placed low on the ground under frosted glasses, the Infanta's nymph-like attendants, all thinly clad after the example of her Royal and nimble self, were glancing to and fro, visible one instant and invisible the next.

Royal gardens were designed for the entertainment not only of a royal family but also of a large court. During festivals and celebrations, large crowds were usually admitted to a palace's environs. At Queluz, festive crowds were diverted by aviaries filled with rare birds, a menagerie of wild animals and a botanic garden containing rare tulip and camphor trees that was entered through a chinoiserie gate. A favourite diversion was a boat ride on an elaborately tiled decorative canal. The canal's inner walls still boast maritime scenes carried out in blue-and-white tiles by the tiler Joao Nunes, while the outer walls have country scenes executed in polychromatic tiles which were ordered from another well-known tiler of that period, Manuel da Costa Rosado. Lord Kinnoull, British Envoy Extra-ordinary to the Infante Dom José, remembered seeing one night after a fireworks display three gaily decorated galleons with actors dressed in allegorical costumes floating down the canal. He also recorded that music was provided by an orchestra playing from a music room which had been constructed on a bridge spanning the water.

The canal fell into disrepair and the music room collapsed in the nineteenth century, but the canal was restored by the great tiler José Maria Pereira Cão at the request of Dom Carlos I (d. 1908). Dom Carlos also had a copy of Giambologna's *The Rape of the Sabine Women* erected on the bridge in place of the vanished music room.

Europe is full of grand formal gardens of this period, but many of them are quite dull. The exceptions are those like Queluz where some special quirk of mind or temperament has been at work to give them life and interest. In Ovid's great book, *Metamorphoses*, the classical writer describes the mythical grotto where Actaeon surprised the goddess Diana in the process of taking a bath:

> Deep in its inner shade, there was a sacred grotto made by no art but by Nature imitating art. Out of the living rock and the light tufa Nature had formed a natural waterfall where the shining water made slender sound and widened from its narrow noisiness into a broad quiet pool surrounded by grassy banks.

Ovid's fable provided a sculptural theme for many of the eighteenth-century's great garden grottos and cascades. Those at the royal palaces of La Granja in Spain, Caserta near Naples and Caxias in Portugal are well-known examples. The elaborate cascade at Caxias is fed by water which is conducted from a hill some distance away to a reservoir on a nearby property. From there it is taken by aqueduct over a public road to the rustic temple on top of the cascade and then down over the many-caved grotto to a pool below. In the pool a stone figure of Diana is shown attended by her nymphs. On the rocks above, Actaeon is depicted already assuming, in punishment, the stag's head. From the other side of the cascade, sculpted hounds are shown baying and baring their teeth. (In the myth, Diana transformed Actaeon into a stag who was then hunted by his own hounds – his punishment for having seen her naked.)

PAÇO REAL DE CAXIAS. A pair of Diana's companions represented in the cascade pool.

This grotto, its garden and the adjoining palace were laid out at the end of the eighteenth century by the Infante Francisco, son of Dom Pedro II and Dona Maria Sofia Neuberg. During the nineteenth century, the palace became a place of resort for both the Portuguese and the Brazilian royal families. It is now an army staff college.

The limestone mountains of the Arrabida peninsula, some 20 miles south of Lisbon, support two distinct types of vegetation. The southern slopes have a heath-like cover of low pine and cypress with an undergrowth of aromatic evergreens such as cistus, lavender, juniper and rosemary. The vegetation, the deeply indented rocky coastline, the blue sea, and the ochre and white colours of the limestone outcrops are more typical of a Mediterranean than an Atlantic landscape. The English traveller Lord Carnarvon wrote in 1936 of riding 'through hills fragrant with lavender and rosemary and finely clothed with olive, pine and cork trees'. Robert Southey, the English poet, wrote of his visit: 'Never did I behold scenery so wild and so sublime... The gum cistus was the most common plant, it was luxuriantly in bloom and the sun drew forth its rich balsamic fragrance.' By contrast, the northern slopes, although now much encroached upon by vineyards, orchards and olive groves, was once a natural forest and a favourite royal hunting ground.

The simplest of tracks through these woods leads to the palace of Calhariz, the seat of the Duke of Palmela. It was built as a hunting lodge by Dom Francisco de Sousa, an ancestor of the present owner, who married Helena of Portugal in 1684. Although it retains much of its character of that period, it was extensively remodelled in the early nineteenth century by the 1st Duke of Palmela. He served as Portugal's ambassador in London for many years where he was a friend of both the Prince Regent and William Beckford. He was also an admirer of the fashionable Regency Neo-classical taste which sought to revive interest in the architecture and design of ancient Greece and Rome.

Many Portuguese *quintas* are obviously no more than summer retreats. Calhariz, by contrast, is in every way a grand ducal seat. Inside the gates the ambience is that of an English park. The trees are smaller and the grass more parched, but there is the same sense of broad expanse, with no fences or hedges in sight. Instead of deer, one may glimpse a herd of goats with bells clinking around their necks as they stretch up the twisted tree trunks, looking for fresh leaves.

The house, the Casa do Calhariz, is not especially grand but the large courtyard and cluster of outbuildings beyond heighten the patrician feeling. The sense of formality is increased by the high iron railings enclosing a *cour d'honneur*; these are punctuated by the gate-piers and by balusters carrying classical busts. Opposite the house is a large fountain pool for watering the horses.

An unusual feature of Calhariz is that all the main rooms are on the ground floor, as is evident from the arrangement of the windows and the central doorway. And the windows are all French, as if the whole ground floor of the house could be thrown open at an instant. The architecture is simple: plain whitewashed stucco and simple pilaster strips at the corners. The single flourish is the entrance portal, with its twisted Salamonic columns and a broken pediment emblazoned with the family coat of arms.

The main entrance opens directly into a large, square, baroque hall rising the full height of the house; a sloping ceiling fills the roof space. The stone chimneypiece is surmounted by a spectacular sculptural overmantel executed in white-painted plaster. In the centre is a full-size figure of Diana the Huntress with a crescent in her hair. In true baroque fashion, her spear stands out beyond the bounds of the frame and real chains are attached to the collars of her hounds, instances of the seventeenth-century's love of realistic theatrical effects. All the marks of a great noble patron are here – polychrome marble busts of Roman emperors on pedestals as well as displays of pikes, tapestries, antlers and oriental pots. The antlers are displayed not on stuffed heads but on life-size wooden sculptures of stags.

CASA DO CALHARIZ. The full-size plaster figure of Diana the Huntress in the entrance hall. She is surrounded by spears, sheaves of arrows, hunting horns and other emblems of the chase.

What is extraordinary about the hallway at Calhariz is the sheer mixture of decorative techniques. The large stone flags set in a diamond pattern on the floor contrast sharply with the blue and white dado. Here there are no pictorial scenes but, simply, huge swirls of acanthus. Behind the stags, the wall is frescoed with a tantalizing glimpse of trees in a park framed by a balustrade and a rich red and gold pelmet. The ceiling above is stencilled with elaborate ornamental patterns – first, acanthus scrolls painted on a rich claret red and, then, a stylized trellis of vine leaves in a faded amber colour.

The second great feature of Calhariz is the *enfilade* of rooms along the garden front. The doors of all eight rooms stand in line; when they are open, a vista of the whole length of the house is revealed. Every room features blue-and-white tiled panels with painted scenes copied from antique engravings and prints.

The culmination of a visit to Calhariz is the chapel, reached by way of a little courtyard at the end of the *enfilade*. It is designed with a tall square nave opening into a chancel that is almost equal in size; it is lit by large lunette windows set into the arches of the ceiling vault. Beneath a tiled scene in one corner of the chapel which portrays St Jerome in the Wilderness is a tiled skirting decorated with playful cherubs and carrying the date 1696. As befits so noble a house, the altarpiece is particularly ambitious, filling the entire end of the chapel. It is executed in highly elaborate marble inlay with twisted columns and triple pediments.

The garden front of the house presents an aspect very different from the others. A great series of terraces, which is higher than the house itself, towers over the formal gardens below. The façade of the house is clad in blue-and-white tiles to the height of the French windows, with stone seats characteristically built into the wall. These tiles are newer than the house, dating from about 1730. Steps at the end of the upper terrace lead down to a lower terrace with a central arched grotto flanked by scrolls of grotesque proportions. From here, a double staircase leads down to a box parterre which is vast, simple in design and in perfect scale with the distant mountains. Although highly intricate, the box pattern can be resolved into three large box squares, two with a fountain at the centre and one with an urn. On the next level below the parterre is another pool of an overall trefoil shape, each petal being extended into a further trefoil to form a series of bold curves which, as Russell Page noted in 1935, 'swing in and out, holding a wide water mirror to the sky'. In a recess of the garden is a Neo-classical stone temple, its shallow dome supported on Doric columns and with a bold inscription in the frieze.

CASA DO CALHARIZ. White-painted plaster, decorative stonework, glazed wall-tiles and unglazed terracotta roof-tiles combine to make a typical combination of architectural materials in southern Portugal.

These many contrasts and harmonies – between the house and its setting, the orderliness of the garden and the wildness of the landscape, the classical temple and its surrounding groves of trees – create at Calhariz a unity of architecture, garden and landscape unique in Portugal.

The district of Lumiar, east of Lisbon, has long been famous for its villas and gardens; those belonging to the Palmela family have always been pre-eminent. In 1875 the horticulturalist Edmund Goetz described their magnificent estate of 125 acres as a horticultural paradise. As late as 1958, Anne Bridge and Susan Lowndes, in their guide to Portugal, were able to describe the entire district as a kind of 'Palmela family suburb, full of exquisite houses, large and small, all belonging to various members of the great ducal family'. Since then, because of Lisbon's growth, the area has been covered with skyscrapers and criss-crossed by motorways. However, two of the Palmela palaces and gardens survive, together forming a pleasant oasis known as the Parque do Monteiro Mor. One of the palaces is now a theatre museum set amid a formal box garden. It was used in the eighteenth century as a residence of the Monteiro Mor, or keeper of the royal forests and hunting preserves. The other palace, known as the Palacio Palmela, is approached through a superb entrance court framed by six *Magnolia grandiflora* and is now a costume museum.

The Parque do Monteiro Mor stretches along the valley between the two houses. One of Portugal's prime ministers, the 3rd Marquess of Angeja, a keen amateur botanist, started the garden in 1793. In 1840, the estate was bought by the Duke of Palmela, another keen amateur botanist. With the assistance of a Belgian called Rosenfelder from the Jardin des Plantes in Paris, he created the romantic garden in the English style that we see today. After Rosenfelder's death in 1844, Dr Friedric Welwitsch, a Viennese doctor and botanist, became the new director. However, in 1853, he went to Angola at the request of the Portuguese government which was anxious to learn more about, and to exploit if possible, the vegetation of its great African colony. During his eight years in Angola, Welwitsch discovered many plants new to science, including the small tree of the Namibian desert, *Welwitschia mirabilis*, which was named after him and which is remarkable in that it survives solely on the moisture provided by the desert fog. The vacancy caused by Welwitsch's departure from Palmela was filled by Jacob Weiss, another horticulturalist from Paris's Jardin des Plantes. His tenure of thirty years saw the garden rise to the peak of its fame.

Today the park comprises an area of 37 acres, of which 20 are gardens and woodland and the remaining 17 devoted to agriculture. In its rapidly changing environment, the park retains a rustic character eloquently described in the last century by the romantic writer Almeida Garret (1799–1854) in his long poem called after the district, *O Lumiar*.

Another, but later, landscaped collection of plants can be enjoyed at the Estufa Fria, an agglomeration of lath houses and greenhouses in the Edward VII park in Lisbon. A disused quarry was converted in 1902 into a semi-tropical garden by the architect and painter Raúl Carapinha. Extended in 1926 and again in 1957, it makes an enchanting place in which to wander on a hot summer's day when the entire complex's airy silence, strange greenish light and fresh, verdant foliage give welcome respite from the noise, heat and dust of the city outside.

QUINTA DA BACALHOA. The main loggia is decorated with a series of five allegorical polychrome tile-panels from the sixteenth century. This one represents the River Mondego.

QUINTA DA BACALHOA. A second allegorical tile-panel represents the River Nile.

QUINTA DA BACALHOA. A third represents the River Euphrates.

QUINTA DA BACALHOA. A fourth represents the Danube.

Opposite QUINTA DA BACALHOA. The new dining-table on the loggia overlooking the garden. In the background is the dado containing the allegorical tile-panels.

QUINTA DA BACALHOA. The tiled entrance staircase leading from the forecourt to the principal rooms on the first floor.

QUINTA DA BACALHOA. A fountain with a quatrefoil basin occupies the centre of the box parterre.

Opposite PALÁCIO DE FRONTEIRA. The elegant, precise geometry of this box parterre mimics the patterns of ornamental tilework.

Above PALÁCIO DE FRONTEIRA. The complex composition of the tile-embellished water tank can be appreciated from the first floor *loggia* of the palace. The statuary along the terrace (the King's gallery) and the staircase balustrades may have been added at a later date.

Left PALÁCIO DE FRONTEIRA. The busts along the Gallery of Kings are set into niches faced with what are known as lustre tiles.

Opposite PALÁCIO DE FRONTEIRA. The Italianate garden front of the palace seen here framed in the portico of the King's Gallery.

Opposite PALÁCIO DE FRONTEIRA. Originally designed as an open loggia, the gallery is decorated with *trompe-l'oeil* paintings of a bird and plant-filled conservatory.

Right PALÁCIO DE FRONTEIRA. On the dining-table is a centrepiece in French empire style together with crested porcelain from Portugal's Vista Alegre factory. In the background is a portrait of the 2nd Marchioness of Alorna dressed as Diana the Huntress.

Below PALÁCIO DE FRONTEIRA. A late eighteenth-century domed ceiling in the south tower. The central plaster figure, representing the Greek goddess Pallas Athene, is surrounded by painted panels of pastoral scenes.

Left PALÁCIO DE FRONTEIRA. The scroll-edged pool before the garden grotto is reminiscent of the scroll-edged pools seen in the Moghul gardens of India.

Below PALÁCIO DE FRONTEIRA. The elaborately ornamented wall that protects the Chapel Walk, enhanced by the flowers of a Judas tree.

Opposite PALÁCIO DE FRONTEIRA. The figure of the flaying of Marsyas, one of a set along the Chapel Walk which was restored by Rocha Correia at the beginning of the twentieth century.

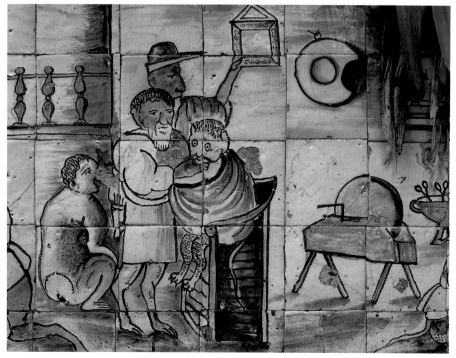

Above PALÁCIO DE FRONTEIRA. A tile-panel in the garden depicts an amanuensis writing a love letter on behalf of a masked client

Left PALÁCIO DE FRONTEIRA. A humorous tile-panel depicting a cat in a barber shop is part of a set by the garden grotto.

Right PALÁCIO DE FRONTEIRA. The Hall of Battles contains tile-panels representing the military engagements of the Wars of Restoration which recovered Portugal's independence from Spain.

CAVALARIA RIPA

TERRIVEL E FVRIOZO COMBATE DE ARRONCHES EM Q CONTEN
DENDO CAVALARIA COM CAVALARIA GANHARAÕ AS INVENCIV
EIS ARMAS PORTVGVEZAS AMAIOR GLORIA VENCENDO E TRIV
NFANDO DO MAIOR NVMERO SEM Q LHE PVDESSE REZISTIR AVE
NIA CÈ DE 1200 CAVALLOS COMO OS CASTELHANOS SE OPPVN
HAÕ A 800 CAVA LLOS PORTVGVEZES SENDO GENERAL
DA CAVALARIA NESTA OCAZIAO ANDRE DE ALBVQVERQVE
DE SAVDOZA ELE VVAVEL MEMORIA Q SOVRE ESHALTAR
NESTE DIA Q SE CONTARAÕ 8 DE NOVEMBRO DE 653 A SVA
FAMA COMO SE VV SANGVE TAÕ GENEROZA MENTE VINGA
DO Q LHE RENDI O AVIDA O CONDE DE ALMARVTE OPRIM
EIRO CABO DAS TROPAS DE CASTELLA COMPERDA DE 400
SOLDADOS E DE 900 CAVALLOS Q SE TOMARAÕ VVOS
L FICARAÕ MORTOS NO CAMPO

PALÁCIO DE FRONTEIRA.
Along a balustrade wall,
the months of the year
are depicted in a set of
blue and manganese tile-
pictures dating from the
seventeenth century.
This one, of December,
illustrates hunters
attempting to trap song-
birds in nearby trees.

PALÁCIO DE FRONTEIRA.
Jupiter and his
thunderbolts are framed
by a garland of flowers in
this tile-picture.

EV·SOV·
OMESTRE
DACOLFA

PALÁCIO DE FRONTEIRA. The picaresque
monkey orchestra of this tile-picture reflects
the late eighteenth-century interest in
singerie, the playful use of the monkey as a
motif in decoration.

PALÁCIO DE FRONTEIRA. Note the brilliant yellow
of the cavalier's coat in this tile-picture.

Left QUINTA DAS TORRES. The domed water pavilion in the garden resembles those which are known to have been a feature of early Islamic gardens.

Right QUINTA DO CORREIO-MOR. The tile decoration over the kitchen hearth humorously depicts an imaginary cooking scene. This is flanked by further pictures of a stag and of an ox.

Below QUINTA DO CORREIO-MOR. A hilltop view over the baroque composition of the *quinta*'s buildings, gardens and vineyards.

Opposite CASA DO CALHARIZ. The garden's Neo-classical rotunda is appropriately set in the Arrabida's Arcadian landscape of mountains and woods.

Right CASA DO CALHARIZ. The eighteenth-century chapel features a superb inlaid marble altar which is considered to be one of the major works of its type to survive from the Joanine period.

Below CASA DO CALHARIZ. A mosaic of two birds is framed and mounted as a wall decoration.

Above PALÁCIO DE POMBAL.
Recumbent hounds in white marble
are an appropriate subject for the
sculptural decoration of a hunting-
palace garden.

Left PALÁCIO DE POMBAL. An
eighteenth-century polychrome tile-
panel of a hunting scene on the
wall of a garden staircase. The
picture is framed in an elaborate
baroque cartouche and the adjoining
steps are decorated with *trompe-
l'oeil* balustrades. pedestals and vases.

Above

PALÁCIO DE QUELUZ. Steps which weave in and out 'like a dancing master's arabesques', lead down to the sunken garden known as the Garden of Malta.

Left

PALÁCIO DE QUELUZ. The palace's garden front which, though classical in its overall inspiration, is ornamented with much delicate rococo detailing over the windows and doors and in the central pediment.

Above PALÁCIO DE QUELUZ. The Azulejos Corridor, which was used as an ante-room to the Ambassadors' Hall, is decorated with fantastical representations of Portugal's colonies on tilework painted by Francisco Jorge da Costa.

Right PALÁCIO DE QUELUZ. Dom Jose's bedroom is plainly designed yet sumptuously furnished, its masculine quality underlined by the avoidance of the gilded and painted furniture which characterizes the Queen's bedroom.

Left PALÁCIO DE QUELUZ. The pilastered walls of the Queen's Bedroom are enriched with late rococo detailing in Neo-classical style. Mirrored panels on walls and doors give a light and airy ambience to the room

Above PAÇO REAL DE CAXIAS. The great rocky cascade with the sculptural group representing the goddess Diana and her companions surprised by Actaeon while taking their bath.

Opposite PALÁCIO DE QUELUZ. The Dining Room in which delicate painted decoration and mirrored doors underline the pavilion-like ambience of the palace. On the left is a buffet designed for the display of china and plate.

AUGUSTO IOANNI, FIDELISSIMO PRINCIPI
REGENTI, LUSITANAE GENTIS SPEI, AMORI,
AC DELICIIS, OB PACEM DESIDERATAM, INNUME
RASQUE RES, CALAMITOSIS TEMPORIBUS, NON
TANTUM ARMIS IMPERII AB OMNI AEVO SEM
PER INVICTIS, SED ET SAPIENTIA, PRUDENTIA,
ET IUSTITIA, ANIMI SUI REGII OPTIMIS VIRTU
TIBUS, FELICITER, PRAECLARISSIMEQUE PERA
CTAS, MARCHIO MARIALVAE HOC MONUMENTUM
C. ANNO   M.DCCCII.

SINTRA

NEAR THE WESTERNMOST POINT of continental Europe and facing directly out to sea are the mountains of Sintra. Covered with luxuriant vegetation and rising sheer out of the plain, they give an impression of grandeur far beyond their size. In Portugal's long history of seafaring no landfall has been more celebrated in its poetry and prose than these mountains. For example, the sixteenth-century poet Gil Vicente describes Sintra in his poem *The Triumph of Winter* as 'a great lady, an enchanted wilderness, and a magnificent landmark for hunters, fishermen and mariners'. In such well-known literary works as *The Lusiads* of Camões or the *História Trágico Máritima*, sailors lost at sea speak longingly of home and the sight of the Ermide da Pena, the highest point of the Sintra mountains. Foreign poets have also been enchanted. The English poet Lord Byron, for example, describes the mountains as part of his epic poem *Childe Harold*.

Three towns – São Pedro, Sintra and Colares – ascend the hillside. The ruins of earlier centuries, such as a Moorish castle, ancient houses, even monks' cells hollowed out of the volcanic rock, are scattered about. Sixteenth-century convents, eighteenth-century manor houses, nineteenth-century villas in exotic architectural styles, even two royal palaces, attest to the mountains' popularity as a summer resort over many centuries.

The mountains are best explored on foot. Narrow lanes lead from manor house to manor house, past town and church. Although high walls often shut out the view, there are tantalizing glimpses of towers and summer-houses as well as of a wealth of architectural detail along the way – shrines and fountains, arches and seats, bridges over sparkling streams. Higher up, paths break out on to the bare, boulder-strewn higher slopes.

The air is pleasantly cool in summer when evening breezes blow in from the sea wafting heady scents of jasmine and myrtle which mingle with the perfume of orange, heliotrope and rose blossom. Because Atlantic rain clouds are intercepted by the mountains, the climate of Sintra is damp and conducive to luxuriant vegetation. Thus the limbs of ancient oaks are thick with fern and moss and provide a deep, sometimes

Previous page PALÁCIO DE SETEAIS. The triumphal arch built by the Marquis of Marialva to link the palace's two wings.

Below QUINTA DO CONVENTO DO CARMO. An overview showing the *quinta* which was adapted in the nineteenth century from a seventeenth-century convent.

impenetrable shade. The ground is carpeted with crocus, scillas and daffodils in spring, and with acanthus and fern in summer. But variety of foliage is provided by other trees: ash, walnut, willow, and both umbrella and maritime pine. Many of Sintra's trees come from exotic areas of the world. Pepper trees from South America, mimosas from New South Wales, eucalyptus from New Zealand all add their distinctive tint and tone. South-facing walls are covered by sheets of wisteria in spring and blue plumbago, bougainvillea and geranium in summer. The geraniums often make thick hedges which are covered with masses of pink, white or mauve bloom in season.

Tucked into a wooded fold of the Sintra mountains is the early sixteenth-century Torre de Ribafria, a pivotal building in the history of Portuguese architecture because it incorporates both late medieval and early Renaissance elements in its design. Unlike many houses of this period, its history is well-documented. Both it and the house which is known as the Casa dos Ribafrias in the town of Sintra were built by Gaspar Gonçalves, a man of humble origin who rose from his position as royal gatekeeper in 1517 to be governor of Sintra in 1569. When the Torre de Ribafria was completed in 1541, Dom João III made Gonçalves the Senhor de Ribafria. Although the Sintra house was sold in the eighteenth century, the Torre remained in the family until 1860.

Due to its solid medieval architecture, with its tower and crenellated parapets, the exterior of the house has an imposing austerity. However, its monumental quality is relieved by the set of graceful windows with delicate columned mullions which run the full length of the house's central section and which establish it, in part, as of early Renaissance design. During the 1960s the house was meticulously restored by Jorge de Mello with the help of his architect, Vasco Regaleira.

Two Sintra manor houses have origins even earlier than Torre de Ribafria. The original structure at Quinta do Convento do Carmo was built by Frei Constantino Pereira in 1465. Two centuries later it became a convent for the Barefoot Carmelites but it was converted into a house after the order was disbanded in 1843 by the Marquess of Pombal. However, the convent's chapel of Sao Pedro still defines the house's overall configuration. Two of the original cloisters have been converted into the present patios of the house with a design that is somewhat reminiscent of the courtyards of the Alhambra in Spain. Also a monk's cell in one of cloisters has been converted into a small oratory, now highly decorated with much gilded carving on a sumptuous red background. Against a dark setting of maritime pines on the uppermost terrace of the garden is a monumental water tank of extraordinary rococo design which was also constructed after the convent had been converted into a secular manor house.

The Quinta da Capela, also located near the small town of Colares, was built in the sixteenth century. However, of the original building only the chapel with its Manueline-style ceiling survived the great Lisbon earthquake of 1755. The present house, built almost immediately after the earthquake, is simple and almost provincial in style. It looks out over a walled garden of open, box-edged beds, the configuration of which is interesting because it echoes the unusual alignment of the overall site.

The Cadaval family, which owns the Quinta da Capela, is descended from Nuno Álvares Pereira, the hero of the Battle of Aljubarrota in 1385 which ensured Portugal's independence from Castile. The family's estate once stretched over most of the western slopes of Sintra's mountains. In 1770 the 4th Duke of Cadaval commissioned the Quinta da Bela Vista, a house on a site with a spectacular view towards the sea. The recessed entrance to the U-shaped house has a flight of stone steps which is panelled in polychromatic tile-work. Its principal room is double height and suffused with light from high-level windows. The walls, which are hung with red brocade, are dominated by a portrait of the 1st Duke of Cadaval. In the garden is a remarkable set of twelve two-faced stone busts. Similar two-faced busts top the pillars of the garden gate at the nearby Quinta Mazziotti, a small eighteenth-century palace at the highest point of Colares.

The most elegant of the late eighteenth-century interiors of Sintra are those of the Quinta de São Sebastião, which enjoys a remarkably well-protected position considering that it stands in the middle of a busy town. From the rear, it is beautifully sheltered by handsome trees, while the ground in front falls steeply away, providing a stupendous view across the old town to the extraordinary beehive chimneys of the old Royal Palace. By contrast with the town's narrow, bustling streets, the spacious, sunlit terrace on which the house stands induces an immediate sense of calm and relaxation.

The house has an engaging charm reminiscent of the *pavilions* or small summer retreats built in the environs of Paris during the same century. In form it is a simple box, pretty rather than stately, which is nicely set off by the plainer building behind which contains offices and servants' quarters. There is no grand staircase leading up to the front door, no imposing central entrance; instead there are six pairs of French windows all opening directly on to the terrace. The architecture is the playful mix of classical and Gothic often found in similar Portuguese buildings of the period. The French windows are all surmounted by pointed arches inset with Gothic tracery. Above these are false oval windows suggesting tall, cool rooms within. Instead of a balustrade along the roofline there is a solid parapet that gives the house a casket-like appearance; the parapet is decorated with a plaster pattern of waving ribbons.

QUINTA DE SÃO SEBASTIÃO. The pavilion-like character of the *quinta* is underlined by its French windows and their Gothic-style lunettes, together with the *trompe-l'oeil* oval windows. The solid parapet is lightened by a relief pattern of twining ribbons.

Tantalizingly little is known of the house's history. It is said to have been built between 1780 and 1786 for the Conde da Póvoa, and its marvellous frescoes have been attributed to the Frenchman Jean Pillement or his school. The decorative painting is indeed of exceptional quality and interest. It was common at this time to paint each reception room of a house in a different style – rococo, chinoiserie or Gothic. With the advent of the Neo-classical taste, scenic landscapes also came into vogue for interior decoration. São Sebastião in all of these respects was abreast of the current taste.

The French windows of the main façade open into two lofty salons of equal size; the salon on the left is painted with a scheme of slender decorative pikes, stood vertically against the wall like billiard cues, while the ceiling is decorated with a repeat pattern of coronets. The adjoining salon manifests the same love of spindly, attenuated forms. Here the slenderest of painted colonnettes carry obelisks and vases in a distant echo of the Pompeian and Etruscan rooms fashionable in France at this time. In both rooms, highly architectural console tables with pier-glasses above stand between the windows.

The most delightful of the interiors is undoubtedly that of the dining-room. It is painted to give the feeling of a garden pavilion, its curtains having been drawn back to reveal a series of landscape scenes behind. This is *trompe-l'oeil* at its most engaging. Every fold of the curtains, as well as their cords and tassels, is painted with exquisite care. The room's shining mahogany table and sabre-leg chairs are pure English Regency in style.

Another room takes up the favourite Neo-classical theme of the primitive hut. It is depicted here as a kind of open verandah supported by tree trunks that hold up a grass roof. The verandah's balustrade seems to be made of crossed branches while the painted landscape in the distance is appropriately luxuriant. Even the chimneypiece is integrated in the painted scheme with crossed logs and straw in the grate. Such rooms are found in many countries in Europe at the time, some directly inspired by the voyages of Captain Cook and deliberately Polynesian in feeling.

The decoration at São Sebastião, whoever may have created it, is a marvellous example of the Portuguese capacity to absorb stylistic ideas and techniques; it is all the more splendid in that it has survived in such excellent condition.

On rounding a sharp bend in the road leading out from Sintra town to Monserrate, one catches a first glimpse of the house of Seteais across a broad stretch of lawn. Upon closer inspection, this building proves to be not one house but two: a pair of matching pavilions. In the centre is a massive triumphal arch in the form of a *gloriette* framing the view. Beyond this, there is nothing more than a flight of steps ascending to a terrace with a panoramic view over miles of lush farmland and its little villages to the Atlantic coastline.

The Seteais estate was bought in 1783 by the Dutch consul, Daniel Gildemeester, one of a group of foreign merchants brought to Portugal by the prime minister, the Marquess of Pombal, from whom he obtained a monopoly of diamond exports. A notable account of Seteais has been left by the English connoisseur and writer William Beckford, better known as the builder of Fonthill Abbey, a prodigy house in the neo-Gothic style in his native Wiltshire. On 25 July 1787, he came to a reception at Seteais and observed tartly that 'the space before the new building is in sad disorder. The house has little more than bare walls. In several of the apartments – you will hardly believe me – one woeful

Opposite QUINTA DE SÃO SEBASTIÃO. The pastoral scenes of the dining-room's frescoes are revealed behind painted curtains. Every fold of the curtains as well as their cords and tassels are painted with great care. Corner console tables support partly gilded bronze candelabra.

candle depended from the ceiling in a solitary lantern. I leave you to represent to yourself the effect of this stable-like decoration.' But Beckford warmed to the entertainment and to the attentions of Mrs Gildemeester. 'There was a bright illumination, a profusion of plate, a striking breadth of table, every delicacy that could be procured, and a dessert frame fifty or sixty foot in length, gleaming with burnished figures and vases of silver flowers of the most exquisite workmanship... the old Consul stood behind our chairs the chief part of supper, handing us the choicest fruits of his extensive gardens, and the best Cape wine I have ever tasted.'

When Gildemeester died in 1793, the property and the consulship passed to his son Daniel who sold Seteais in 1800 to the 5th Marquis of Marialva. It was the latter who, in 1802, built the second matching pavilion and the triumphal arch in honour of the then Prince Regent, the future King João VI.

The most unusual feature of Gildemeester's *quinta* – built in the mid-1780s – is that it is without a trace of baroque or rococo detail. Here is pure Neo-classicism of French inspiration. Ornamental detail is pared to a minimum; the emphasis is on ele-

QUINTA DE MONSERRATE. A boldly projecting cornice emphasizes the cylindrical shape of the *quinta*'s pavilions and the contrasting cube of its central pavilion. Its setting was created by the landscape painter William Stockdale.

gance of proportion. Chasteness and understatement have replaced the architectural exuberance of the 1770s. The house has an engaging domesticity: the front entrance is simple and modest; there is no palatial flight of steps. The upper rooms, lit by small square windows, are self-evidently low and intimate. But the house is given an imposing quality by the solid parapet with its impressive urns.

The later triumphal arch, by contrast, has much more swagger. It bears a massive raised attic containing the dedication, and above this a blaze of carved military trophies. Moving around to the side of the house, one notices that the architecture becomes plainer, without the shallow panels which provide modelling to the entrance front. Here, on the terrace, is a good place to sit and enjoy one of the most glorious of Sintra's many views. On a clear day, the wooded mountainside is shadowed by the fairytale silhouette of the royal castle of Pena; from the other end of the terrace, one can see a topiary garden with huge spheres and cubes of neatly clipped box packed in between the lower box hedges.

The interior of the house was extensively remodelled and redecorated when it became a hotel in the early part of this century. Furniture, upholstery and decorative painting have all been marshalled to form a delightful ensemble in every room, and one pretty blue-green drawing-room has walls and ceilings painted with a continuous landscape open to the sky. The overall result is an amazing tribute to the survival into this century of traditional Portuguese craftsmanship.

Few country houses have elicited more passionate reactions than those which have been built at nearby Monserrate. In 1811, Lord Byron declared the house at that time to be 'the most desolate mansion in the most beautiful spot I ever beheld'. For the English author Rose Macaulay, 130 years later, the present house was dismissed as of a 'barbarous orientalism constructed in a Moorish delirium'. Yet many visitors have come away enchanted, as they still do, as well as fascinated by Monserrate's association with two famous Englishmen William Beckford and Sir Francis Cook, the Victorian millionaire art collector.

In 1540, there was a chapel here, built by Gaspar Preto, the superior of the hospital of All Saints in Lisbon. During the seventeenth century, the property passed to the Mello Castro family. Shortly before 1790, it was acquired by the English merchant Gerard de Visme (1726–98). Of Huguenot background, he had emigrated to Portugal at the age of twenty. In 1793 he completed the first house at Monserrate in a style described by Beckford as 'barbarous gothic'. Two prints depicting 'Mr. de Visme's country seat at Monserrate drawn by Noel, engraved by Wells, 1795' show a fanciful building in the castle style with three towers in a row which, despite subsequent alterations, remains the basis of the house as it is today.

Beckford, in spite of his reservations about the house, was sufficiently captivated by the beauty of the landscape to rent the property in 1794. He had described it on a previous visit as 'a beautiful Claude-like place surrounded by a most enchanting country'. With the help of a carpenter from Falmouth in Cornwall, he began to make improvements to the house and garden. He wrote to Sir William Hamilton, the famous antiquarian and husband of Lady Hamilton, of 'my proceedings here, building and gardening etc.' He wrote to a Portuguese friend: 'I have been engaged with the Royalty of Nature, with climbing roses and cork trees, with tracing rills and runnels to their source, and examining every recess of these lovely environs.' Before returning to England in 1795, he had opened several paths through the woods, one leading to a natural cataract, another to the sixteenth-century chapel. These continue to form one of the bases of the present landscape layout.

Both Beckford and de Visme had returned to England, leaving Monserrate abandoned, when it was occupied by French troops during their invasion of Portugal in 1807. Its subsequent forlorn state was characterized by Lord Byron in his poem *Childe Harold* (1811):

> Thy fairy dwelling is as lone as thou!
> Here giant weeds scarce a passage allow
> To halls deserted, portals gaping wide.

More than three decades later Edward Quillinan found the place even more desolate: 'The house is a temple for the winds....', he wrote. Yet he found the grounds 'still exceedingly beautiful, with sloping lawns... sparkling, leaping, roaring waterfalls, silent pools, gardens and orange groves, stately trees and wooded, park-like sward.'

By good fortune, Monserrate fell into the hands of a new owner who would revive it. Sir Francis Cook (1817–1901) was the son of a linen draper who dealt in all types of woollen and cotton goods, silk and linen and built up a successful manufacturing and distributing business. Cook came to Portugal in 1841 and later married the daughter of an English merchant there.

Cook acquired the lease of Monserrate in 1856 and some two years later commissioned the English architect James Knowles Senior to reconstruct the house using an English building contractor, James Samuel Bennett. The style adopted was a Moorish Gothic – one of the most extravagant kind using a wealth of luxuriant carved detail which was, in any case, a hallmark of Knowles' style. In its overall composition, Monserrate is an exceptionally vigorous composition. The bold, projecting cornices give it strong, clean lines and emphasize the cylindrical shape of the towers as well as the contrasting cube of the central pavilion. The octagonal dome and the circular cupolas on the towers are rich in colour and even slightly fussy in detail, but this only increases the sense of the exotic.

Today, Monserrate remains in good condition, but it has a haunting quality because it is completely empty. On ascending the steps to the main loggia, one continues along a terrace which encircles the house. So exotic is the architecture both inside and out that there is a temptation to pause and peer through every window. The rich tracery of the loggia, with horseshoe arches set with pointed arches, offers a foretaste of what lies within. Everywhere one layer of ornament is superimposed on another. The *tour de force* is the long broad corridor that runs down the centre of the house, framed by a procession of arches that produce dramatically alternating shafts of brilliant light and deep shadow. Every wall surface is a frenzy of incised ornament, and the treatment continues across the ceilings. This frantic ornamentation reaches its climax in the circular music room, where each pointed arch is enclosed by a larger one – an inner niche and an outer one, with upper and lower arches in the main arcade of columns that encircles the room. The cornice is enriched with spiky crests and hanging pendants; the dome is overlaid with panels of swirling tracery.

Cook lavished equal attention on the gardens, commissioning the romantic landscape painter William Stockdale to compose scenic vistas from the house. Long,

QUINTA DE MONSERRATE. Humour is never very far from Portuguese garden decoration. Here, a stone trough is ornamented with an applied table setting, the spoon being placed unexpectedly on the lower rather than the upper side of the plate.

sloping tree-framed lawns were created, one descending to a lake which forms a focal point on one side of the house. A circuit walk was threaded through the woods, linking a new avenue bridge with the cataract and chapel, and passing through groves of camellias and tree ferns, the latter now among the tallest growing in Europe. Cook bought some carved stone pillars and an Etruscan sarcophagus in Rome in order to make the chapel ruins look more picturesque. The windows and doors of a secluded stable building were faced with panels of cork bark, a traditional type of decoration best exemplified at Sintra's sixteenth-century Capuchin convent.

Cook asked William Nevill of the Royal Botanic Gardens at Kew to select and position a collection of rare plants in the garden. Plantings of Lusitanian cypress were added to the indigenous oak and chestnut woods, while sweeps of hydrangeas soon enriched the existing shrubbery of laurel, pittosporum and myrtle. Crinums, belladonna lilies and agapanthus were planted into the wild carpet of fern and acanthus that in summer succeeds springtime's colourful bluebells, scillas, grape hyacinths and crocus.

Arum lilies colonize damp depressions while swamp cypress, banana and bamboo produce subtropical visual effects around the lake. A palm collection of 25 species is displayed on a slope below the bridge. Tall Norfolk Island pines break the skyline, and the rounded heads of huge New Zealand Christmas trees break into crimson flower each July. Clumps of aloe, Australian flax and doryanthes make busy focal points around the house, while the Cape honeysuckle and a violet-blue twiner from western Australia, *Hardenbergia comptoniana*, climb luxuriantly on the pillars of the colonnade. But most impressive are the huge specimens of the New Zealand kauri pine, *Agathis australis,* and the relative of the camphor tree, *Cinnamonum burmanii*, its new leaves graded in shining crimson, orange and acid green.

These plant collections eventually ran to more than three thousand species. They were cared for by a succession of English gardeners including Walter Oates who wrote a detailed account of them in the *Gardeners' Chronicle* in 1924. However, in 1946, the Cook family sold the notable contents of the house and the estate was transferred to the Portuguese state.

Situated on a hill that is crowded with exotic villas in various architectural styles, the Quinta da Regaleira stands out as the most elegant fantasy of them all. It was conceived by an Italian, Luigi Mannini (1846–1936), an architect and stage designer who was a native of Brescia. He worked at the La Scala opera house in Milan before coming to Portugal in 1879 as a designer at the Sao Carlos opera house in Lisbon. From set design he expanded into the design of theatres, working on the theatre at Funchal on the island of Madeira. Exhibition design also became one of his specialities; he designed the Portuguese pavilions for a number of the world fairs and international exhibitions held in the Americas around the turn of the century. His architectural career reached a peak in 1888 when he was asked to design the new royal palace at Bucaco in central Portugal.

His client for Quinta da Regaleira was Carvalho Monteiro (1850–1920), a man with an immense fortune who was a passionate collector, particularly of shells, butterflies, clocks and silver and who was for many years president of the Lisbon zoo. His presence is still felt throughout Regaleira: his initials are carved on a window by the front door; stone carvings of his wife and three grandchildren peer out from under a window overlooking the garden, and carvings of his dogs stand guard by one of the stable doors.

Throughout Europe at this time, it was considered patriotic to revive historic national styles of architecture and decoration for use in modern buildings. For Portugal, this meant the revival of its own distinctive form of Gothic called Manueline – after King Manuel whose reign (1495–1521) marked the summit of Portugal's supremacy at sea. The style was characterized by abundant sculptural decoration incorporating both vegetative and marine motifs. Branches of laurel and oak leaves, corn-cobs, artichokes and acorns as well as anchors, ropes, pearls and terrestrial globes were all frequently used. The fact that Quinta da Regaleira looks from some points of view as if it might be the chancel of a long-vanished Manueline cathedral is a tribute to its architectural success and that of the team of sculptors from Coimbra who worked on it.

The principal entrance to the estate is itself an elaborate architectural fantasy that stretches along the road for upwards of a hundred yards. Loggias, galleries, balconies and terraces are arranged along its length as if by a stage designer planning the exits and entrances of a large body of characters in a play. The serpentine drive winds upwards to the house and its chapel, and then on upwards again through the estate's woods. Swans inhabit rock pools in woodland nooks. A bath-house and a fountain are provided for refreshment, ornamental seats for rest. One of the seats is decorated with carved figures of storks, another with lions, yet another with greyhounds.

As the drive reaches the top of the hill, the sculptural ornament becomes deliberately rougher in treatment. The drive enters a gloomy defile which is crossed by a series of rock-work bridges and where at one point is located a huge boulder. This swivels on a concealed pivot to give access to a well shaft plunging into the shadows below. Around it, an arcaded gallery spirals downwards to a network of underground passages which lead along past further top-lit well shafts and swan grottos – a journey designed to induce a kind of sublime terror in the visitor. Progress along the caverns is by the light of a hand-held candle and the squeaking and fluttering of colonies of bats heighten the dramatic effect. This strange experience provides a fitting climax to a tour of a house and garden which were conceived in a mood of extravagant romanticism. The last private owner of Regaleira was Fernando d'Orey who imported many plants for the garden from Madeira. His daughter-in-law, Tisha d'Orey, carries on the family's traditional interest in gardening to the present day.

The last of the Cadaval family houses to be built in Colares is the Quinta da Piedade. Constructed in the nineteenth century, it was used for some time as a local market house before 1935 when the Marquis of Cadaval, brother of the 9th Duke, restored it as a house. Among the house's collections of paintings is a portrait of Nuno Álvares Pereira, one of Portugal's fourteenth-century high constables and a great national hero.

The gardens created by the Marchioness of Cadaval face inwards towards the mountain. The gardens of the early 1900s were often influenced by the simple formal gardens of the fifteenth and sixteenth centuries, the period before gardens became large and complex in design. Their simplicity struck a chord in the minds of those who were laying out gardens for a new and simple age. A system of laying out small garden 'rooms' was devised which could be adapted to any size. Like the rooms of a house, each garden 'room' could have a different colour scheme or character and they could be grouped to form an *enfilade*. The garden of Quinta da Piedade is one of the few Portuguese gardens laid out in this style.

The first room has a blue-tiled summer-house presiding over a formal rose garden. The second room is in the form of a camellia garden set around a fountain basin in the shape of an eight-pointed star. To one side of this room is a pergola walk, its inner wall faced with large tile-pictures. To the other side is the music pavilion which was the setting for many of the concerts organized by the Marchioness. The next room in the main sequence is the swimming-pool garden, beyond which an open pergola of modernist design frames distant views and from where a winding path descends to a hedged *potager* or kitchen garden. This is the last garden room of the sequence. In all, the garden is an excellent example of the adaptation of the traditional features of a national style of gardening to fit a new and simpler age.

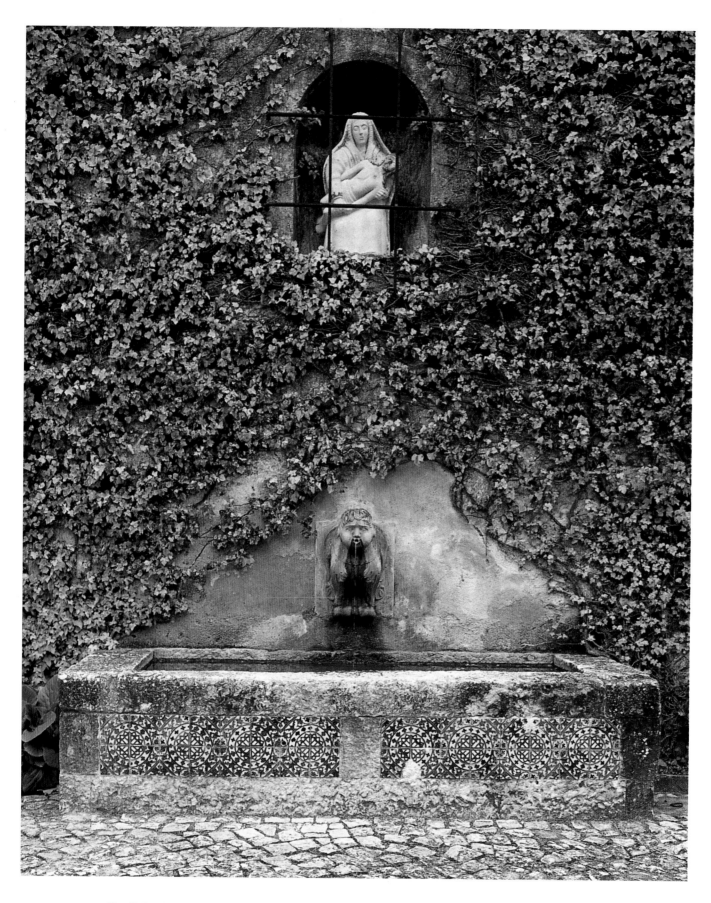

TORRE DE RIBAFRIA. The tiled wall-fountain in the external wall of the building is under the protection of the Virgin in the niche above.

TORRE DE RIBAFRIA. Massive fortress-like walls are relieved by carefully trained ivies and clipped box hedges.

Above TORRE DE RIBAFRIA. The main
approach and entrance into the *quinta*'s
courtyard which is protected by walls
with crenellated parapets.

Right TORRE DE RIBAFRIA. A domed
canopy protects the courtyard cistern
which is decorated with diamond-shaped
tiles laid in a chequerboard pattern.

Opposite TORRE DE RIBAFRIA. The picturesque
agglomeration of buildings in the rear courtyard has
another tiled wall-fountain as its focus.

QUINTA DE SÃO SEBASTIÃO. The salon's wall frescoes
simulate an open-air enclosure bounded by skins
stretched between tall slender poles or lances.

Above QUINTA DE SÃO SEBASTIÃO. The decorative sentry box on the *quinta*'s terrace. In the background is the old palace of Sintra with its pair of astonishing kitchen chimneys.

Opposite QUINTA DE SÃO SEBASTIÃO. The frescoes of the dining-room depict pastoral scenes in the style of the French artist Jean Baptiste Pillement.

QUINTA DE SÃO SEBASTIÃO. The Manueline windows and bottle-shaped chimneystacks of the old palace of Sintra as seen from the *quinta*'s terrace.

QUINTA DE SÃO SEBASTIÃO. A garden pot is finished with a chequerboard glaze. Glazed garden pots are appropriate in a hot climate as their surface reflects rather than absorbs heat

Opposite QUINTA DE SÃO SEBASTIÃO. Glazed lunettes over the doors underline the pavilion-like ambience of the interior. The sabre-leg chairs, some of which are lyre-backed, are in a pure Regency style.

QUINTA DE SÃO SEBASTIÃO. A veiled view from the house towards the building designed for offices and servants' quarters.

Left QUINTA DE SÃO SEBASTIÃO. A pair of doorways between the two salons allows the guests to circulate freely. The archways have double doors and the lunettes above them are glazed in a pattern repeating the tracery of the *quinta*'s French windows.

QUINTA DE SÃO SEBASTIÃO. The vaulted ceiling of the salon is stencilled with a Neo-classical composition which includes coronet, fan and honeysuckle motifs.

Opposite QUINTA DE MONSERRATE. A fountain with a figure of a triton stands before the entrance, which is located in one of the *quinta's* drum-shaped pavilions.

Left QUINTA DOS FREIXOS. A tank is ornamented with a rococo figure holding a lyre. A wisteria flowers in the background.

Opposite QUINTA DE
MONSERRATE. Richly carved
foliate traceries, cusped arches
and octagonal flower-beds are
based on the architecture and
decoration of the Moors who
occupied southern Portugal for
many centuries.

QUINTA DE MONSERRATE. The
rustic wall finish is in
deliberate counterpoint with
the finely executed carving of
the window surround.

Left PALÁCIO DE SETEAIS. The blue-green salon in which walls and ceilings are frescoed as one continuous landscape open to the sky in a clever twentieth-century pastiche of Jean Baptiste Pillement's eighteenth-century fresco style.

Opposite PALÁCIO DE SETEAIS. Integrated interior decoration is displayed in the precisely fitting console table, the swan-necked legs of which are repeated in the painted fresco behind.

Below PALÁCIO DE SETEAIS. A fresco detail from the principal saloon – a mermaid and merman ride a seahorse through the waves.

Opposite PALÁCIO DE
SETEAIS. The palace
archway frames a distant
view of the hilltop
nineteenth-century royal
palace of Pena.

PALÁCIO DE SETEAIS. An
oblique view over the
box garden and
cylindrical summer-
house below.

Left QUINTA DA PIEDADE. The twin-sashed windows in the garden pavilion are an exceptional form of fenestration in central Portugal.

Below QUINTA DA PIEDADE. The brilliant autumnal colour of virginia creeper enlivens the entrance steps and portico of the roadside *quinta*.

Above QUINTA DA PIEDADE. The flowers of hibiscus, bougainvillea, Cape honeysuckle and lantana, together with the blue-tiled seat, provide a rich mixture of colour against the sober greens of box and cypress.

Right QUINTA DA PIEDADE. Stone cherubs playing musical instruments ideally complement a garden in which many famous garden concerts took place.

Above QUINTA DA PIEDADE. Antique harps, a beautifully decorated Tasken harpsichord and a lampshade inscribed with musical notation testify to the Marquesa de Cadaval's interest in classical music, of which she has been an outstanding patron.

Left QUINTA DA PIEDADE. Over the chimneypiece in the salon is a painting of an ancestor of the Cadaval family, Nuno Alvares Pereira, hero of the 1385 Battle of Aljubarotta which ensured Portugal's independence as a nation from Castille.

SOUTH OF
THE TAGUS

ALMOST HALF OF THE GEOGRAPHICAL AREA of Portugal lies south
of the Tagus river. In the past, it has been characterized by the great size of its landholdings and by a widely scattered and sparse population. Its manor houses, whether they be
in the early Manueline style or in later eighteenth-century baroque style, are invariably whitewashed, and their simple geometric forms are emphasized by the strong southern light.

The late fifteenth-century Torre de Águias is set high on a hill surrounded by olive
groves in a remote corner of the Alentejo, as the region south of the Tagus is known.
Once the seat of the Counts of Atalaia, it stands 72 feet high, is laid out on a quadrangu-
lar plan and with four floors separated by ceilings of ribbed vaulting. Unlike the contemporary towers of northern Portugal, it has a considerable number of windows as well as two
chimneys, indicating that it was meant to be continuously inhabited even through the cold
Alentejo winters.

In a less commanding position amid the olive and cork trees of the hills of the northern Alentejo is the sixteenth-century manor house of Paço da Giesteira. Above it, and to
the west, is the great fortress of Monteiro-Novo, site of many battles against the Moors who
occupied Portugal during the early Middle Ages. The house's unique significance is in
the survival of many architectural features from the Mozarabic period – that is, the brief
period after the Reconquest during which the Moorish architectural style was still used
in Christian Portugal. Its survival is particularly significant in the Alentejo where many early
manor houses have disappeared because the building materials often used were fragile. Its
survival is even more remarkable in that it lay empty and little-maintained after its confisca-
tion during the Portuguese revolution of 1974. However, in 1986, it was restored to the Cus-
todio da Avó family. Of even earlier origins, but with many major modifications dating from
successive centuries, is the greatest house of the Alentejo, the palace of Vila Viçosa.

VILA VIÇOSA

By the beginning of the fifteenth century, the Braganza family, which hailed from northern Portugal, had established a residence at Vila Viçosa within striking distance of Lisbon. From it in 1640, Duke João de Braganza set out to assume the throne of Portugal at the end of the period of Spanish domination. Today, it is in every sense a royal palace of European rank, whether for the majestic extent of its façade, the labyrinthine complexity of the rooms or the richness of decoration from every period of its history.

The long main front is in a severe Renaissance style devoid of decorative flourishes. All the architectural detail is in low relief with little emphasis at the centre and none at the ends. The use of pilasters to divide up the façade rather than columns adds to the flat effect, and the austere monotony is increased by the use of identical windows on each floor for the whole length of the façade. It faces on to a vast empty ceremonial square and the entire effect is softened only by the warm colour of the façade's Monte Claro stone.

The oldest part of the palace that can be seen today is the early Renaissance courtyard completed for Jaime, 4th Duke of Braganza (1479–1532). It is surrounded by an elegant single-storeyed arcade with columns in an archaic, almost Romanesque style. The full Renaissance style was introduced in the expansion carried out to the palace by Teodosio, the 5th Duke of Braganza (1508–63). Particularly interesting are the schemes of decoration undertaken by him in the large open staircase leading to the apartments on the first floor. The walls are covered by huge frescoes painted in 1537 in imitation of tapestries and depicting one of the glorious events in the history of the House of Braganza, the taking of Azamor by Duke Jaime. These frescoes are fascinating in the detailed information they provide about contemporary arms and armour. The infantry wear coloured stockings and striped doublets. Most carry pikes or long spears; only a few are equipped with muskets. The handsomely embossed cannons are shown with their original wooden gun carriages, which rarely survive today; the wheels are edged in metal to give them greater strength. The Duke looked not only to Italy for inspiration in the decoration of his newly expanded palace but also to Holland, importing a fine series of Dutch tiles portraying the biblical story of Tobias, which are emblazoned with the ducal arms and dated 1558.

Of the next scheme of decoration, which was initiated by Duchess Caterina (1560–1614), wife of the 6th Duke, João I, only two rooms survive. One, the Sala de Duquesa, has a very flamboyant ceiling, the panels of which are painted with red and gold arabesques on a white ground. The narrow barrel-vaulted oratory in the palace also dates from this time. It was described by Cardinal Alexandrino in 1571 and has a ceiling painted with grotesques in the manner of Raphael's Vatican loggias.

The 7th Duke, Teodosio II (1568–1630) initiated the present great façade, which took nearly two centuries to complete. Inside, major decorating schemes were carried out in advance of the Duke's marriage in 1603. These included the adjoining rooms, the Sala de David and the Sala de Medusa. The Sala de David, also known as the Giants' Room, takes its name from the elaborate illusionistic paintings on the high-coved ceiling. The scenes of David are portrayed on conventional canvasses set into elaborate decorative panels with *trompe-l'oeil* sculpture groups in the corners. Below the ceiling is a painted frieze inset with oval mythological scenes. The tiled dado has been documented by dos

Previous page PAÇO DE VILA VIÇOSA. The German Hall with a set of two eighteenth-century Gobelins tapestries illustrating the story of the Misfortunes of Porus. The ceiling is painted with early eighteenth-century portraits of members of the Braganza family, the earliest ones being conjectural works.

Above PAÇO DE VILA VIÇOSA. The ceremonial façade facing the square is divided by light-relief pilasters in a manner based on the façades of Roman palaces such the Farnesina and the Palazzo della Cancelleria.

Santos Samoes, the great authority on Portuguese tiles. Executed in geometric patterns of a strong blue colouring, the tiles are comparable to a series in the ancient palace of the Dukes of Infantado in Guadalajara in Spain. For the latter an order survives, dating from 1595, to the master tilemaker Fernando de Luayza working at Talavera de la Reina. In 1602, Luayza received, in the name of his son-in-law Juan Fernandez Oropesa, another commission from the high constable of Castile for 'certain houses of his'. This high constable was none other than Juan Fernando de Velasco, the father of Duke Teodosio's Spanish bride.

Also part of the marital redecoration is what is known as the Sala de Medusa with a fine tiled dado also attributed by dos Santos Samoes to the manufactory at Talavera de la Reina. The tiles are painted in blue and white on a yellow ground with classical

PAÇO DE VILA VIÇOSA. The carving of the Renaissance chimneypiece in the Medusa Room is somewhat two-dimensional, which suggests it was made in Portugal from an Italian pattern-book.

herms, scrolls of acanthus and inset landscape panels portraying fortified towns. Each group is enclosed by a key-pattern border with a simulated egg-and-dart moulding. The fireplace, its overmantel elaborately carved, is in the contrasting black and white marbles which were in favour at the end of the sixteenth century in northern Europe (Duke Teodosio's Spanish bride would have been familiar with Flemish taste as Holland, at that time, formed part of the Spanish Netherlands). Again, the ceiling is as ornately treated as any in a contemporary Italian palazzo; it is divided by curving ribs into a series of panels illustrating the legend of Perseus and Medusa. These panels alternate with large medallions painted with grotesque ornaments on a white ground.

These grand rooms, laid out on either side of a central staircase, form part of an impressive *enfilade* creating a vista through the entire length of the palace. Each door is set exactly in line with the preceding one from one end of the palace to the other. This is an early example of a palace with such a layout and reflects the fact that the Iberian peninsula, with its elaborate court etiquette, played a significant role in the development of palace planning in Europe. The first Spanish example of the characteristic baroque arrangement of paired apartments, one for the noble proprietor and one for his wife, opening off either side of a central staircase or hall, was seen at the Royal Palace in Madrid.

On the other side of the staircase from the rooms described above are two further rooms redecorated for the marriage of Duke Teodosio in 1603. The first, the Sala das Virtudes, served during the seventeenth century as the Duke's wardrobe. This has an octagonal panelled ceiling with ribs prettily painted in pink and gold and inset with full-size female figures portraying the virtues. The next room is the Sala de Hercules, named from the painted scenes of Hercules' labours. It has a very handsome Renaissance chimneypiece, the design of which was apparently based on engravings published in Serlio's *Architecture*. It is supported on herms with an elaborate frieze of *putti* or cherubs playing soldiers. In this room is hung a magnificent set of Brussels tapestries executed from cartoons by Rubens and dating from *c.*1630–5. Opposite these hangs another fine set of seventeenth-century tapestries of German and Italian manufacture.

As kings of Portugal, the Braganzas continued to remodel and redecorate the palace during succeeding centuries. Foremost in doing so was that great patron of the arts, Joao V, in the early eighteenth century. The grandest room in the palace is known as the Sala dos Tudescos, which takes its name from the German guard of honour first recruited for the dukes in the sixteenth century. It is dominated by a massive gilt ceiling inset with a series of brilliantly colourful portraits of the Dukes of Braganza. These are the work of Giorgio Domenico Dupra (1689–1770), an Italian painter from Savoy, who had studied in Rome and painted the exiled Stuarts. There he was noticed by the Marquis of Fontes, King Joao's ambassador, whose famous state coaches are in the Coach Museum at Belem. In 1719, the Marquis brought him to Portugal, where he spent more than ten years. The portraits of the first eight dukes were modelled on existing portraits or engravings with impressive results. However, the greatest flourish is naturally reflected in the portraits done from life, notably those of Joao, 14th Duke of Braganza, and his young family.

Another of Joao's redecorations can be seen in the chapel at the back of the palace wing. It attained its present dimensions in about 1728. The barrel-vaulted ceiling was inset with decorative painting suggesting the influence of the early eighteenth-century

PAÇO DE VILA VIÇOSA. Queen Amelia's Bedroom with its striped, tent-like ceiling and its unusual nineteenth-century plane-wood furniture.

Opposite PAÇO DE VILA VIÇOSA. A Moorish-style fountain and box pattern which were formed during the garden's re-creation.

engravings of Jean Berain. The palace kitchen, with its bold baroque arches, dates from this period of renovation as does the palace coach-house.

Queen Amelia later made a bedroom in the palace wing which is of interest; it is hung with striped silk to emulate the interior of a tent and now contains an attractive set of late nineteenth-century plane-wood furniture. The Sala de Jantar (the dining-room), although dating from 1785, has today an unmistakably nineteenth-century character. The elaborate parquet floor was added by Queen Maria II about 1843, but the most striking feature is the set of chandeliers; this parallels the antler furniture which was so popular a feature of central European country houses and which had been introduced to England at Osborne House on the Isle of Wight by Queen Victoria at the time of the Great Exhibition in London in 1851. The antler chandeliers at Vila Viçosa serve as a reminder that near the palace extends the great Braganza Chase, a walled hunting park of 5,000 acres, the largest in Portugal.

The palace yard and gardens enjoyed perhaps their greatest moments in the period before 1640, the year in which Spanish rule in Portugal was ended. The palace was a focus of Portuguese nationalism; the Duke held what amounted to an independent royal court there, organizing great festivals, princely marriage feasts, theatrical performances and, on occasion, bullfights in the ceremonial square. To enable members of the court, particularly the ladies, to watch the festivities in the square from the privacy of the palace gardens, twelve windows with built-in seats and protective decorative grilles were opened in the wall of what is known as the Duchess's Garden. The garden itself takes the form of a shady promenade along which the Duke, his Duchess and the royal household would take the air on a summer evening. It is planned like an outdoor gallery. Along its length are arranged no fewer than 50 built-in garden seats, each accompanied by a flower-bed raised to eye and nose level so that the sitter might enjoy the sight and scent of the flowers at very close quarters. A further sixteen seats and their accompanying flower-beds are arranged at the end of the promenade around a pool where the sitters might enjoy the refreshing atmosphere provided by the fountain's spray. Further still, an ornamental doorway based on an engraving by the Italian architect G.B.Vignola (1507–73) leads into a grotto and a small *patio*, a covered arcade and a suite of rooms to which the royal couple might retire if the garden itself became too crowded with promenading courtiers.

Many of the early gardens of the Iberian peninsula contained enclosures set aside for the exclusive enjoyment of the household's ladies – evidence, perhaps, of lingering Moorish tradition. At Vila Viçosa, the Ladies' Garden now contains three groups of four box-edged beds, each group set around a low fountain unmistakably baroque in its shape but equally unmistakably Moorish in its height and scale.

During the centuries of Braganza rule in Portugal, the palace of Vila Viçosa was retained as a family rather than an official home. When Manuel II, the last of the Braganza kings, died in exile in 1932, the palace and its contents were bequeathed to the nation for use as a museum. Since then, successive and thorough restorations have created the arrangement of the exterior and the interior we see today. Both are impeccably maintained.

The early baroque house of Quinta de Nossa Senhora do Carmo was built during the late seventeenth century by King Joao IV for a lady of his court. Set in the rolling border country of the eastern Alentejo, its long, single-storeyed structure is dominated by a much higher chapel to one side. Its simplicity of style, horizontal proportions and contiguous fenestration are typical of the Alentejo's domestic architecture. Its interior, with its coloured tiles and richly wrought wooden panelling, is, by contrast, unexpectedly luxurious.

Formal house planning of the seventeenth century was based on the unit of the 'apartment', that is, a set of rooms – ante-room, saloon, bedroom and closet – arranged in a sequence according to increasing privacy of use. Unusually, the garden of Quinta do Carmo is laid out according to the same principles: its four outdoor spaces are arranged in order of increasing privacy. A pair of rococo stone figures flanks the gate from the road into the first of these spaces – a gravelled courtyard between two ranges of service buildings. It leads into a second space, the entry court of the house, which is divided up into a series of grass squares. From here a stone gate, decorated with urns, niches and a coat of arms, and almost hidden under a huge wisteria, gives access to the third space in the sequence. This is a densely planted, walled area which is criss-crossed by walks, some of which are shaded by elegant lattice-work. Steps lead up to the final space, the 'closet' of the outdoor 'apartment' which is almost entirely occupied by a balustraded water tank with a figure of Neptune in the centre. Behind the tank is a small grotto-like summer-house ideal for intimate summer banquets.

The Casa do Marques de Alegrete located in the town of Elvas offers an excellent example of the white-painted interiors of the region, which are often enriched by blue-tiled dados, gilded picture and mirror frames, and colourful textiles and are also often enlivened by gleaming silver and sparkling chandeliers.

Until the recent advent of tourism, the Algarve, the southernmost province of Portugal, was also its poorest on account of the general infertility of the soil. This, combined with the region's traditional susceptibility to earthquakes, has left it with few monumental buildings and gardens. Even the houses of the province's nobility, though often large, are simple in design with a minimum of decoration. An exception to this austerity of architectural character is the palace of Estói, 8 miles north of Faro, the Algarve's provincial capital.

The original house was built in the eighteenth century by Francisco Jose Moreira Pereira Carvalhal e Vasconcelos (1756–1823) next to the small whitewashed village of Estoi. After a period of neglect it was bought in 1893 by Jose Francisco da Silva, later 1st Viscount of Estói, who set about its remodelling. The palace now belongs to the municipality of Estói.

In Portugal, as elsewhere in Europe, the late nineteenth century was a time of historical revivalism in architecture and garden design. The neo-baroque was favoured as a 'luxury' style and was often adopted by those who wished to proclaim both their wealth and political conservatism. Following this path, the future Viscount of Estói assembled a team of Portuguese experts in neo-baroque decoration that included the architect and decorator Jose Francisco da Silva Meira, the decorative painters Maria Baretta and Adolfo Greno, and the tile designer and maker Pereira the Younger. With their assistance, the previously plain façade of the house was enlivened by the addition of a

Opposite QUINTA DE NOSSA SENHORA DO CARMO. The entrance gate, flanked by a pair of welcoming figures, frames a view of the *quinta* and its chapel glistening white in the Alentejo summer sun.

parapet balustrade punctuated with urns and statues, high-level *trompe-l'oeil* windows, an ornate first-floor balcony and a tiled arcade at ground-floor level. All these embellishments had the effect of making the house façade resemble some theatrical confection conceived by a *fin de siècle* scene painter.

The garden rivals the house in the intricacy of its neo-baroque detail. The first of the three terraces in front of the house has four large flower-beds arranged around a central stone fountain which depicts a sportive boy riding a dolphin. The planting in the beds today is of mixed shrubs and perennials. Cycads, montbretias, dimorphothecas and chrysanthemums are outlined against the geraniums and Cape honeysuckles that climb the garden's enclosing walls. A modestly robed Venus as well as sentimental figures of a peasant boy and girl alternate with neo-baroque urns in an arrangement which is set against illusionist tile-paintings along the base of the house wall.

The middle terrace of the garden is reached by a bridge over a dry moat. A double staircase then descends around a grotto with three arched openings filled with tinted glass to reveal in the dimly lit interior an elaborate representation of the Life of Christ. The staircase walls themselves boast a scheme of decoration in which carved figures of reclining nymphs are set against painted tile panels illustrating lush, subtropical landscapes. A motley assembly of life-like busts, including heads of the German statesmen Bismarck and Moltke, and of the poets Schiller, Goethe, Milton and Camoes, add to the sense that the whole design might be that of a stage-set for some late nineteenth-century operetta by Offenbach or Meyerbeer.

A group of white marble nymphs spill water from their upturned pots into a balustraded pool which fills much of the centre of the terrace. At one end, in the shade of tall trees such as a Queen palm, *Syagrus romanzoffiana* and a Canary Island date palm, *Phoenix canariensis*, is an enchanting wrought-iron bandstand complete with a set of matching chairs and music stands. This acted as a focal point for the garden parties fashionable at the time.

The lower terrace is reached by another double staircase faced with large-scale blue-and-white tiles. It encloses a grotto in which stands a copy of Canova's subtly erotic sculpture of *The Three Graces*. With the delicate pebble-and-shell mosaic decoration on its walls, the grotto exudes the effeteness and femininity characteristic of much *belle epoque* decoration. On the other hand, to the side of the house, a raised columned terrace in imitation of a ruined classical temple proclaims a more sober Neo-classical architectural style.

Entering this sleeping beauty of a garden today is like parting a veil on an untouched turn-of-the-century world; it seems to be awaiting a cast of characters in period costume to walk in and bring it back to life.

PAÇO DE VILA VIÇOSA. In this simple traditional closet, nineteenth-century neo-baroque gilt furniture has been reupholstered with pink fabric to match the dress of the Infanta in the oil portrait.

PAÇO DE VILA VIÇOSA. The state dining-room with its stuccoed ceiling dates from 1785, though its present furnishings, including the antlered chandeliers, date from the nineteenth century.

Left PAÇO DE VILA VIÇOSA. Royal portraits and splat-back baroque chairs furnish the Medusa Room. Its dado, with medallions illustrating romantic rural scenes, was commissioned in the seventeenth century by Duke Teodosio II.

Opposite PAÇO DE VILA VIÇOSA. A gilded cherub holds aloft the lace canopy of a royal cradle.

Below PAÇO DE VILA VIÇOSA. A detail from one of the Gobelins tapestries in the German Hall. The ceramic vase is sixteenth-century Italian.

Above PAÇO DE VILA VIÇOSA. Military uniforms are cleverly displayed in a closet of a bachelor's bedroom which is decorated in a masculine straightforward style.

Right PAÇO DE VILA VIÇOSA. The Mannerist painted decorations are among the most important to survive in Europe. The frescoed battle scene on the staircase depicts the successful siege by the 4th Duke of Braganza of the city of Azamor in Morocco.

Opposite PAÇO DE VILA VIÇOSA. In later centuries, the Braganzas continued to use the palace as a royal hunting lodge. Collections of nineteenth-century furniture and pottery commemorate this period.

Right PAÇO DE VILA VIÇOSA. French Aubusson tapestry and late eighteenth-century gilded and tapestry-covered chairs furnish the room known as the Salon of the Prince of Brazil.

Below PAÇO DE VILA VIÇOSA. Nineteenth-century royal portrait photographs form a kind of family shrine around a gilded and ebonized piano of the same period.

Opposite PAÇO DE VILA VIÇOSA. The barrel-vaulted ceiling of the oratory is completely covered with grotesque paintings of outstanding quality.

PAÇO DE VILA VIÇOSA. The grand kitchen of the palace, with its bold baroque arches, dates from 1728.

PAÇO DE VILA VIÇOSA. The palace's irregular rear façade is focussed on this whitewashed double staircase to the garden.

Opposite CASA DE ÁGUA DE PEIXES. The arris window with horseshoe-shaped arch in Manueline style is one of the house's many important early architectural features.

QUINTA DE NOSSA SENHORA DO CARMO. A rustic wall grotto is
deliberately constructed with rough-cut stones and decorated with
much-pitted tufa rock.

Opposite   QUINTA DE NOSSA SENHORA DO CARMO. Neptune presides over
the balustraded pool in the most secluded part of the garden's layout.

Left QUINTA DE NOSSA SENHORA DO CARMO.
The dining-room furniture is in a sober English
baroque style. In the background, tilework
pictures of bucolic scenes, one of which
depicts an informal bullfight, are set in
architectural frames featuring *trompe-l'oeil*
capped urns and console brackets.

Above QUINTA DE NOSSA SENHORA DO CARMO.
The cool effect of tilework in Portuguese
rooms is often offset by the warm tones of
mahogany or gilt furniture.

Above QUINTA DE NOSSA SENHORA DO CARMO. Hardwearing materials such as stone and tile characterize the traditional Portuguese country kitchen. Note the recessed stone basins and the traditional flower-painted country kitchen ware.

Left QUINTA DE NOSSA SENHORA DO CARMO. This tile-panel depicts a classical ceremonial triumph in which the victor of war returns laden with booty. Womenfolk celebrate with incense, music and laurel leaves.

Opposite QUINTA DE NOSSA SENHORA DO CARMO. A recessed china cabinet with bold gilt rococo framing. Over the Chippendale-style chair is a wall clock with a magnificent Neo-classical lyre-shaped pendulum.

Opposite CASA DO MARQUÉS DE ALEGRETE. The richly detailed wall-panelling is constructed using a complex mix of materials and colours.

Right CASA DO MARQUÉS DE ALEGRETE. Behind the newel post of the main staircase, a tiled dado is composed of pictures representing hunting scenes.

Below CASA DO MARQUÉS DE ALEGRETE. The whitewashed walls, white-painted chairs and white lace cloths which are typical of an Alentejo house are enlivened by sparkling glass, gleaming silver and a mirror reflecting light into the interior of the dining-room.

Left PALÁCIO DE ESTÓI. Nymphs spill water from their upturned pots into a balustraded pool which is located along the garden's central perspective of terraces.

Below PALÁCIO DE ESTÓI. The horizontal line of the terrace wall is broken by a rhythmical arrangement of marble busts.

Above PALÁCIO DE ESTÓI. A child and a dove, symbols respectively of innocence and peace, accompany the goddess Flora, seen here adorned with floral garlands in her hair.

Right PALÁCIO DE ESTÓI. Marble figures and terracotta pots are set in the blind arcade which stretches along the garden front of the palace.

Left PALÁCIO DE ESTÓI. Flights of steps in diagonal counterpoint, the tile-panels depicting pastoral themes of love. Flowers, musical instruments and a shepherd's crook underscore the Arcadian theme.

Below PALÁCIO DE ESTÓI. A venerable god in white marble is overtaken by the wayward growth and orange flowers of the Cape honeysuckle, *Tecoma capensis.*

THE DOURO

MANOR HOUSES IN THE REGION OF THE DOURO river proliferated in the eighteenth century as a result of a boom in wine-growing activity and also as a result of the construction of a road joining Oporto, at the mouth of the river, with the town of Vila Real in the interior. Most of the larger manor houses with exuberant baroque façades are located along the right bank of the river while the smaller houses of the local gentry tend to be located along the banks of the Tamega, a tributary of the main river.

Many of them have origins older than the eighteenth century. One such is the Casa do Campo Belo situated in Vila Nova de Gaia across the river from Oporto. Its history goes back to the end of the fourteenth century when King João I granted the lordship of Gaia to Álvaro Cernache for services rendered. Its surviving tower dates, however, from the early fifteenth century.

Entered from the street through a gate in a high wall, the courtyard is surrounded by the manor house and its contiguous buildings. Only after passing through the house is the fabulous view of the river and city beyond suddenly revealed – a panorama that is all the more impressive on account of its deliberate concealment until the last moment. In the foreground of the view is a small, traditional box garden laid out around a pool and a promenade walk which leads off to the right. It is lined with seats and a collection of rococo statuary set against a high hedge of the crimson-flowered camellia *Camellia japonica* 'Mathotiana'. At the far end, wide steps lead down to a lower platform on which two famous camellia trees cast their dense shadow over a rustic fountain. Formerly thought to have been imported from Japan in the mid-sixteenth century, these trees are now considered to be only two hundred years old; but, none the less, they are impressive specimens. They are 30 feet in height with trunks which are more than 3 feet in circumference. Each year in February and March, rose-pink flowers cover the trees, later falling to the ground to create a lush pink carpet. Beyond, the walk descends through meadows and woods to the great port wine houses on the quaysides of Vila Nova de Gaia.

Another walk ascends the hill behind the house. Passing under a vine pergola through neatly kept orchards and vegetable gardens, it eventually reaches a wood planted around a freshwater spring. The collection of old trees in this area includes an outstanding tulip tree which is second in size and age only to the well-known specimen at the Quinta do Meio, located directly across the river from the Casa do Campo Belo. The late owner, the 4th Count of Campo Belo and the 16th lord of the manor, worked with his wife to keep up the house and its garden with meticulous attention to detail.

Also with early origins is the Casa do Campo, which looks out over the flood plain of the Tamega river towards the hills of the Serra do Marão. It is modest in comparison with the many imposing manor houses of the region yet it is impressive in terms of the imagination of its architects. It was begun in the late sixteenth century but considerably modified in later centuries so that it is transitional in architectural style, comprising both Renaissance and baroque elements. A rough stone tower with parapets and bevelled turrets at one end of the house develops into a baroque house which is linked by a bridge with a graceful chapel at the far end. The two-winged house, set at an angle, forms an unusual triangular relationship with the arcaded wall of the raised garden. From a distance, the house is partially concealed behind the giant topiary of its garden.

Another house on which construction was begun in the seventeenth century, but which was not completed until the middle of the eighteenth, is Casa de Quintã which stands among groves of scrub pine above the Douro river. Its early commencement date is evidenced by its austere façade, and its late completion date by the light-hearted elegance of its grand double entrance staircase. A similar combination of austerity with rich decoration can be experienced in the interior, especially in the main salon where the undecorated trapezoidal wooden ceiling contrasts with the baroque decorations of the wooden wainscotting.

Also standing among the steep hillsides and sloping vineyards of the northern bank of the Douro stands the Casa de Penalva. This handsome manor house, with a garden and pavilion directly inside its entrance gate, together with its chapel, were built in 1738. The house was much altered in the nineteenth century and the chapel was completely rebuilt as late as 1933.

The elaborate ornament which is a characteristic of the architecture of the eighteenth century can be seen at Casa dos Porto Carreiro and at Solar de Mateus. Standing in a field at the edge of a eucalyptus glade, the incomplete Casa dos Porto Carreiro is one of the most spectacular and scenographic façades in Portugal. The house was commissioned by António de Vasconcelos Carvalho e Menezes, a wealthy noble who had made part of his wealth in Brazil, and was constructed, judging from the shafts of the columns around the entrance door, about 1760. The ornament concentrated on the front of the building can be linked to the work of the Italian architect Nicolau Nasoni (1691–1773), who had such a decisive influence on the eighteenth-century architecture of northern Portugal. The upper windows with their inverted pediments (called *lambrequins*) and simulated curtains, all carved in granite, derive from Nasoni's designs for the gilt woodwork of his churches in Oporto. Such unconventional carved ornamentation as the overscaled shells, the ruffled, asymmetrically composed groups of fruit and flowers which appear on the façade are almost surrealist in the drama and intensity of their execution. In spite of the fact that work on the building was abandoned before its completion and that it is now semi-ruined, what remains at Porto Carreiro forms a wonderful visual composition and a poignant reminder of Portugal's eighteenth-century glory.

SOLAR DE MATEUS

A sun-dappled countryside of vineyards, orchards and chestnut trees heralds the approach to the village of Mateus where the country house of the Counts of Vila Real is situated. The building's unforgettable silhouette, known throughout the world from the label on its famous rosé wine bottle, bristles with pediments, pinnacles and scrolls, thus ensuring it a place among Europe's most extraordinary houses in the baroque style.

SOLAR DE MATEUS. A simple but carefully maintained box garden complements the plainer garden façade of the house. The almost naively carved granite figure of a saint is typical of the provincial school of sculpture which flourished in northern Portugal.

Upon arriving at the estate, there is a short drive to the extensive open terrace on which the house stands. At first glance, the house and its adjoining chapel seem doubled in size by reflection in the large ornamental pool which extends in front of it. The house is completely freestanding and it is possible to walk around it examining it from every angle. The long flanks of the building, immediately intriguing, conceal an inner courtyard. One might easily conclude that this house was planned in every detail by a single architect, but its history, so far as it is known, is more complicated.

There was a house on the site in 1619 but the present building is associated with António José Botelho Mourão who married Dona Joana Maria de Sousa Mascarenhas in 1721. It was evidently finished by 1743 when the archbishop of Braga, Dom José de Bragança, was informed that Antonio José 'had demolished a palace and built a better one'. The chapel, however, which is set back from a rear corner of the house, was added by Dom José's son, Dom Lúis António de Sousa Botelho Mourño. According to an inscription, it was completed in 1750.

Robert Smith, the great historian of Portuguese art and architecture, has attributed the Solar de Mateus to Nicolau Nasoni. In his major monograph on Nasoni's work, he points to a gap in the architect's career between 1730 and 1743 when he could have been working on Mateus. One of the hallmark's of Nasoni's work is the use of highly inventive and exaggerated baroque detail: extraordinary door and window cases, as well as balustrades, inspired by the Italian baroque architects Buontalenti and Borromini. But as Smith has pointed out, the long wings of the house are very much plainer than the exuberant architecture of the entrance façade. This suggests that Nasoni may have been remodelling an earlier building.

In the entrance courtyard, the detail becomes steadily more exotic, reaching a crescendo over the entrance door itself. For example, the second-floor windows on the end of the wings have simple triangular pediments; inside the court, the windows have serpentine pediments that give way to swan pediments over the windows on either side of the front doors. Here Nasoni developed the baroque fascination with convex and concave curves to the full, with stone mouldings surging up and down and back and forth across the façade. The swan pediments contain flat shells that push up the cornice above; by contrast, the shell over the front door is modelled in three dimensions. Above, the roof balustrade first recedes, then ascends; in a final flourish, the balustrade handrail and balustrade base sweep off in opposite directions. Nasoni makes great play with vertical architectural accents and statues. But the signatures of Mateus are the amazing finials, like giant pepper grinders, at the corners of the courtyard. There is a double stair up to the front door and an even more ingenious arrangement is found in the inner courtyard. Here, an arcade at second-floor level is approached by no less than four separate flights of steps. What delights at Mateus is the sheer exuberance of detail in so compact an area.

The love of axiality and symmetry evident in the external composition is evident throughout the house interior. The entrance door opens into a central hall; doors on the right lead into the main range of apartments. These rooms, overlooking the garden, are laid out with an *enfilade* of double doors at the centre, so that, when the doors are open, it is possible to see from one end of the wing to the other. The main feature of all the interiors is the woodwork, especially the ceilings which are of the usual trapezoidal form.

SOLAR DE MATEUS. The entrance hall boasts a richly carved wooden ceiling, magnificent armorial door-curtains or *portière*, baroque hall seats and an elegant sedan chair.

They are magnificently rich and dark in colour, and all the decorative mouldings are immensely bold – indeed, voluptuous. The furnishing, though sparse, is fine: great cupboards and massive beds, all in excellent condition. The careful planning of the interior, so careful and exact, suggests the hand of a skilful architect who has given thought to every detail. If Nasoni was only remodelling the house, the original architect must have been a man of great experience and competence.

The pleasure of a visit to Mateus is completed by its exceptionally well-maintained gardens which descend in a series of box-planted terraces from the house. The first box garden is patterned in a complex series of both round and square beds, each bounded by an unusual combination of inner and outer box hedges, the inner one clipped lower than the other. Bisecting the lower garden is a cypress tunnel. Its glorious barrel vault of feathery cypress foliage, clipped from a specially shaped ladder, is a tribute to the art of Portuguese topiary. The tunnel walk is continued out into the fields under a most elegant pergola, supported by single shafts of granite carved into the form of obelisks which sit on baluster-like pedestals.

On either side of the tunnel are smaller gardens – one a modern water garden presided over by a weeping Japanese maple, the other a more traditional box garden with one exceptional feature – a boundary hedge of such vigorously sculpted form that its shape must have been inspired by an eighteenth-century French pattern book. One might have expected the gardens to have ended there, but the most beautiful box pattern of all lies beyond this hedge. It is focused on a decorative wall-fountain and its pattern spreads out from a central Hinoki cypress, *Chamaecyparis obtusa* 'Nana Gracilis' in a series of scrolls and counter scrolls, arcs, diamonds and arabesques. The corners of the design are filled with representations of the family's coat of arms, also in box. The fluid pattern stands out with exceptional brilliancy against its background of white marble chips.

SOLAR DE MATEUS. A dwarf Hinoki cypress is the focal point of this embroidered parterre. In the background a baroque wall-fountain is flanked by a pair of Italian cypresses.

In addition to this important eighteenth-century house and garden, the Douro river region also has one of the finest late nineteenth-century gardens in Portugal. The idea of a wild woodland garden was first popularized by William Robinson's book *The Wild Garden*, published in London in 1870. His method of planting woodland with flowering trees and shrubs so that they would appear part of a natural setting soon became popular as a way of displaying the colourful new camellias, rhododendrons, maples and hydrangeas that were then flooding into Europe from the United States and the Far East. Because of its strong tradition of formal gardens and also on account of its climate, few woodland gardens were made in Portugal. An exception is the garden of Quinta da Aveleda located between Penafiel and Paredes, 20 miles east of Oporto.

An avenue lined with great evergreen, cork and English oaks, 30-feet-high camellias and evergreen azaleas descends from the entrance gates to end at an elaborate fountain in front of the house. The fountain is known as the Four Sisters Fountain because of its carved portrait medallions representing the four seasons. The avenue turns around the fountain to lead directly to the house, which is in an unusual neo-vernacular Arts-and-Crafts architectural style. Instead of nestling behind the traditional box parterre, the house is surrounded by a series of undulating small-scale lawns divided by winding gravel paths in the manner of the nineteenth-century villa garden. Forest-sized trees grow on them – cedars, swamp cypresses, a tulip tree and a Californian redwood. One of the small lawns has a duck pond with an island on which has been erected a whimsically conceived, half-timbered duck-house with tiers of thatched roofs, each crowned with a traditional straw doll.

The pride of Aveleda is its woodland garden. The tree canopy is mostly of oak which, with its deep root run, high airy crown and rich leaf litter, is an ideal environment in which to grow shade-loving plants. Dappled light falls on to massed camellias, rhododendrons and hydrangeas between which sheets of periwinkles, dead nettles, day lilies, bergenias and ivies cover the ground. Exotic trees such as a ribbon gum, a Japanese cedar and a Norfolk Island pine provide occasional focal points.

A series of follies gives occasional architectural focus to the woodland's varied plantings. The entrance lodge to the estate is a fanciful granite structure with a roof of elaborate thatch. A goat-house takes the form of a cylindrical tower with an external winding ramp on which the goats like to climb. Deeper in the wood is a large pond with islands. On the first stand the remains of a Gothic window rescued from the partial demolition of the birthplace of Henry the Navigator in Oporto. The second island is conceived as an elaborate rocky fountain. The third, reached across a rustic bridge, has a picturesque thatched summer-house. The charming frivolity of the summer-house's architectural details is matched by that of its furnishings and fittings; tables made of mariner's rope and chairs made of a boatman's oars are but two examples.

Nearer the house, a grass terrace leads to a raised granite platform in front of a wall fountain. Also rescued from a local demolition, this baroque structure is decorated with both three-dimensional and relief carvings illustrating that mixture of classical, Moorish and Christian motifs which so aptly reflects Portugal's cultural history. In March, the joints between the granite paving stones are filled with brightly coloured polyanthus flowers which have seeded themselves freely. At the opposite end of the grass terrace is

Opposite QUINTA. DA AVELEDA. From the mask on this granite· wall-fountain shoot sprays of carved foliage to create an image which, in modern parlance, is known as that of 'the green man'.

an aviary, in the style of a Turkish kiosk, housing songbirds that provide a musical background for summer garden parties.

A garden, because it is composed of living plant material, needs to be not only well designed but also well maintained. The daily ministrations of a knowledgeable hand are essential to its well-being. Many well-designed historic gardens in Portugal lack life because this is absent. Not so at Aveleda, where a fine, original design is matched in quality by its present high level of development and maintenance.

Two more modest manor houses are interesting on account of their association with Portuguese writers. The Quinta de Vila Nova, nestling in the extraordinary landscape of the Douro river valley, was in the late nineteenth century the home of the realist novelist Eça de Quieróz. The manor house and its chapel preside over commanding views of the picturesque hills, terraces and vineyards of the valley which are enhanced by its constantly changing colour and light. In the writer's time the house could only be reached on foot by way of a steep path leading upwards from the river and railway station below.

An unusual feature of the Casa de Pascoaes is a glass cubicle, just large enough to shelter one person, that stands on the terrace by the manor house. This cubicle, which contains a stone table and bench, faces the Serra do Marão, the gentle hills beyond the valley of the Tâmega river. It was built by Teixeira Pascoaes (1877–1952), Portuguese poet and man of letters, as a vantage point to be used on dank winter days. Pascoaes loved this landscape, which is said to have inspired the first stanza of *Painel*, a seminal work in twentieth-century Portuguese literature. Immediately to the left of the cubicle is a simple entrance to three remarkable rooms, all panelled in a light, biscuit-coloured wood. No housekeeper has tidied the great profusion of manuscripts, books and old copies of *A Aguia,* the periodical he published in 1910. On the walls, paintings – both oils and watercolours – are stacked, hung and pegged haphazardly. In one room is a remarkable and thoughtful bust of the poet by the noted sculptor António Duarte.

The treasure of these rooms, however, is a huge brightly painted red biscuit tin made by a long-forgotten manufacturer. In it are bundles of letters – the poet's correspondence with many of the great writers of his time: Lorca, Unamuno, Rojas, Cortesao, Pessoa. Most poignant among these letters are some from the Chilean poetess Gabriela Mistral, ten years his junior. Many of her letters are short notes saying: 'I'll be at this address if you want to write to me.' In another room is a narrow bed, a simple washstand, a small round stove and, next to it, a chair with cushions. Here the poet created his own separate, private world within the larger world of the manor house.

Great gardens from the 1930s, particularly in the International or Art Deco style, are few in number, but Portugal is lucky enough to possess one, still in superb condition, at Casa de Serralves on the outskirts of Oporto. It was brought into being by the 2nd Count of Vizela who commissioned a design from Marques da Silva, an architect better known for his design of the new Oporto railway station. With its spare silhouette and minimal decoration, it looks almost like a gigantic wireless cabinet of the period. For the interior of the house, Vizela chose work by three of the greatest furniture designers of the twentieth century: the cabinetmaker Emile-Jacques Ruhlmann, the ironworker Edgar Brandt, and the jeweller and glass-blower René Lalique. For the designs of the

CASA DE PASCOAES. No housekeeper has tidied the profusion of books, manuscripts and magazines on these bookshelves.

garden, Vizela turned to Jacques Greber, a Frenchman who had designed the garden around the Palais de Chaillot for the International Exposition held in Paris in 1937. The house and garden are now seeking new life under the care of the Secretary of State for Culture as Portugal's first national museum of modern art.

QUINTA DA AVELEDA. Legs carved in the shape of anchors and the use of twisted rope for the top give this garden table a maritime design theme.

QUINTA DA AVELEDA. A beautifully conceived thatched rustic summer-house at the entrance to the woodland garden.

Opposite QUINTA DA AVELEDA. A window surround, saved from the demolition of the house in Oporto where Henry the Navigator was born, has been erected on an island in the garden's lake.

Left CASA DO CAMPO. Great topiary 'umbrellas' overhang the courtyard from the terrace above.

Below CASA DO CAMPO. A domed summer-house, formed of clipped camellias and with a stone table and benches inside, provides a cool summer retreat.

Left CASA DE PASCOAES. A view of Pascoaes'
library as he left it when he died in 1952.
Above the heavily laden bookshelves is a
medley of portraits of his friends and fellow
writers. Much of the furniture is of his own
design and, like these chairs with pointed backs,
has many Gothic references.

Above CASA DE PASCOAES. A table in
Pascoaes' study with some of the many
objects he collected which have been left in
the positions they were in when he died.

CASA DE PASCOAES. A typical seventeenth-century northern Portuguese manor house, reconstructed in the nineteenth century, is always vigorous in conception yet sometimes charmingly provincial in execution.

SOLAR DE MATEUS. The garden front of the house is much plainer in design than the exuberant entrance front.

Above SOLAR DE MATEUS. Translucent
autumn foliage complements the smooth
mottled bark of a *Lagerstroemia indica.*

Left SOLAR DE MATEUS. The ornamental
orchard to the side of the house is
divided by paths and clipped hedges.

Opposite SOLAR DE MATEUS. Copper pans are arranged decoratively on the kitchen's fireproof granite walls and ceiling.

Right SOLAR DE MATEUS. The chinoiserie room with a carved oriental figure seated on an elaborate canopied throne.

Below SOLAR DE MATEUS. The bold and magnificently carved overdoor pelmets which are a feature of the interior can be seen in this *enfilade* of rooms.

Overleaf

SOLAR DE MATEUS. A box parterre on a white marble chip background is planted with red salvias, orange marigolds and red lagerstroemias. Note the complex sculptural form of the boundary hedge.

THE MINHO

THE MINHO, PORTUGAL'S MOST HISTORIC REGION, was once one of the most remote on the Iberian peninsula. The Moors did not penetrate north of Braga and few pilgrims to Santiago de Compostela travelled southwards beyond the Minho river. Because brigands roamed the countryside until well into the sixteenth century, few farms or estates became established. Those that did exist were small holdings, no larger than one family might manage.

Established families lived in defensible, fortified tower-houses. Some of these, like the fourteenth-century Paço de Giela, north of the Vez river, still stand, isolated on their commanding hilltop positions. This is one of the few remaining examples of a Portuguese noble residence of the Middle Ages. It consists of an almost windowless tower with high perpendicular battlements and an adjoining but unconnected residential building which boasts a fine Manueline window and an ogival door, all constructed in durable granite. Other towers dating from the fourteenth century, such as the Torre de Aguiã nearby, have been incorporated in later mansions.

The Solar dos Pinheiros from the same period is more of a town house than a country manor. Bordering a historic square in the old Roman town of Barcelos above the Cavado river, its elongated façade between twin towers forms a handsome counterpoint to the collegiate parish church of Santa Maria Maior next door. According to an inscription on the south door, it was built by Dr Pedro Esteves, a canon lawyer and a magistrate of the Braganza lands. While the house has undergone some subsequent changes, its façade, including a pair of original doors and a window with fine mouldings, remains well intact. More elegant but less solid towers dating from the fifteenth century form an integral part of two later country manors in the baroque style – at the house known as Solar de Bertiandos and also at Torre dos Azevedos.

In the middle of the eighteenth century a blight destroyed many French vineyards: as a result wine from Portugal, as well as from many other countries outside France, came into demand and the Minho began to prosper. It was then that many of the region's great baroque houses came to be built. The builders of Paço da Glória near the town of Jolda chose to erect a house that harks back in part to the style of the medieval house, with two towers and crenellated battlements. However, the broad double entrance staircase is a most obvious baroque element and the loggia overlooking the garden clearly reflects Italian influence.

Also partially archaic in style is the early eighteenth-century Paço de Calheiros, set high above the northern bank of the River Lima. Its construction seems to have been started by Jácome Lopes Calheiros in 1700. Although the two towers of the façade seem to echo the fortified towers of earlier castles, the window configuration and ornament is firmly baroque in style, as is the monumental entrance staircase arranged unexpectedly around the highly decorated façade of a family chapel.

Another manor house dating primarily from the early eighteenth century is Casa dos Biscainhos. Now that the town of Braga has grown up around it, it is difficult to imagine its earlier rural setting. Its main façade, according to the historian Carlos de Azeve-do, dates from the seventeenth century when it was commissioned by Dom Diogo de Sousa, the Archbishop of Braga who was responsible for much of the contemporary embellish-ment of the city of Braga. He commissioned Basque workmen from Vizcaya province, who were then working on the cathedral, to begin work on his palace.

The principal entrance was designed to let carriages and other vehicles enter a covered court which forms an entrance to the house as well as a passage to the stables and gardens beyond. From its graceful, stone-paved floor rise arched doorways and granite pil-lars on each of which stands a statue of a small page in eighteenth-century costume. Of par-ticular interest in the palace interior is the state room. A vast empty space, some 43 feet in length, its lower walls are covered with *azulejos* of Coimbran manufacture dated 1724. The ceiling of carved wood is painted with scenes from the life of Beato Miguel de Carvalho of Braga, one of the town's great religious figures. The *enfilade* of rooms run-ning along the garden front is furnished and decorated in nineteenth-century style. The din-ing-room decoration contains scenes painted on canvas which wallow in characteristic nine-teenth-century romanticism. They recount tales of despair taking place in picturesque ruins.

As important as the palace is its garden. It is a remarkable, lovely example of late baroque landscape architecture, with many references to the later *rocaille*. Three terraces descend from the house. The first is bare except for a monumental stone foun-tain with crouching stone figures spewing water from their mouths and carrying on their backs a giant baluster pedestal from the top of which a jet of water shoots high into the air. On the second terrace is a box garden which is surrounded by a unique parapet wall, faced with glittering tiles in blue, yellow and white and with a granite coping of rippling outline that rises like a wave to lap against the high-backed seats and tall gate-piers along its length. One set of gate-piers is capped with obelisks and set at a provocative angle to the wall: another is crowned with stone figures of angels blowing on hunting horns. The box pattern is so complex it is impossible to understand at a glance, yet some of its circular beds do stand out as visual anchors in the otherwise diffuse pattern. All the beds are planted with solid blocks of roses or of annuals such as salvias, celosias, marigolds and cannas in the strong, lively colours which are popular in the public parks of the Minho. The central stone fountain is of tiered shell basins held aloft by mermaids riding on the backs of dolphins. Subsidiary stone fountains are of boys blowing on conch-shell trumpets; two of them are now standing in the shade of living summer-houses formed of giant clipped camellias. The third terrace was – when the English garden designer Russell Page saw it in 1935 – an ornamental orange grove with neat rows of vegetables and paths lined with blue and white irises. Although its planting is now less disciplined, it still retains a singular gazebo – an encrusted grotto at ground level supporting an octagonal summer-house above with elegant tiers of windows above which an onion dome glitters with glazed tiles in a way reminiscent of the tile-clad domes of Samarkand. At the apex of the dome is a quaint, Don Quixote-like granite figure typical of the decoration of many houses and gardens in the Minho. At the bottom of the garden a stone pavilion with flanking colonnades overlooks an enclosure that was once reserved for white peacocks. The Casa dos Biscainhos is today not only an important museum but also a workshop for the teaching of traditional wood-carving administered by the University of the Minho in Braga.

The historic market town of Ponte de Lima is surrounded by many eighteenth-century manor houses of unpretentious elegance. The Casa de Pomarchão, largely reconstructed in 1755 when a chapel was also built, is noteworthy for its long first-floor and ground-floor colonnades which also characterize the Solar de Bertiandos nearby and the Torre de Azevedos. However, all also boast vigorous baroque roof outlines and much other decorative detail. The Torre de Azevedos contains two noteworthy rooms: the grand entrance hall with a pavilion-shaped polychromatic wooden ceiling; and the main tower room decorated with panels of *azulejos* depicting recent events in the lives of the Azevedos family.

Another eloquent example of late baroque architecture is the Mosteiro de São Simão da Junqueira, which is situated east of Vila do Conde and north of Oporto. Dominated by the twin towers of the adjoining parish church, it was constructed around the cloister of an old monastery. The monastery had been built between 1072 and 1082, before Portugal's emergence as a nation, by a Dom Aria, an archdeacon of the nearby town of Braga. From the late sixteenth century, it served a congregation of Augustinian monks who remained there until the prime minister, the Marquis of Pombal, banished religious orders from Portugal in the eighteenth century. Then its life as a secular manor house began. The cloister became the house patio, its walls enlivened by allegorical tile panels thought to be of either Moorish or Sevillean origin. An elaborate box garden depends for water on an aqueduct of considerable height and length, its water serving the house and surrounding vineyards as well. The interior is conceived as a succession of handsome rooms off a corridor above the cloister. Of large and austere proportions, with painted ceilings of carved wood, the rooms are today furnished with simple elegance. Although many of the pieces are of Portuguese or Indo-Portuguese origin, there is also furniture which originated in turn-of-the century Paris. The house contains a remarkable collection of liturgical vestments, of paintings by Grão Vasco, Portugal's great nineteenth-century master, and of early Arraiolos carpets of considerable beauty. All give to this setting the wonderful air of continuity that reflects the long evolution of many Portuguese manor houses.

CASA DE SEZIM. The forecourt with the customary array of gates, bell, lanterns and a *claire-voie* surmounted by a granite urn which is planted with a drought-resistant yucca.

Situated near another Augustinian monastery at Leça do Bailio, north of Oporto, is another late eighteenth-century summer house, the Casa dos Cónegos. Some of its baroque decorative details are so exaggerated that it may be possible to attribute them to the imagination of the highly inventive architect Nicolau Nasoni, who is known to have designed the Quinta do Chantre nearby. Nasoni's style was often so extreme as to prefigure the decadence and decline of the baroque style which was to be succeeded by the more refined rococo and more simplified Neo-classical styles.

Towards the end of the eighteenth century the arcadian baroque style which gives its architectural character to much of the Minho area was being replaced by a lighter rococo, and later to a more restrained Neo-classical style. The Casa de Sezim, about 3 miles south of the handsome, bustling town of Guimaraes, exemplifies both styles. As one approaches, the house is visible from a distance, halfway up the side of a hill: its long lines and low, pyramidal roofs give it an oriental look. The house's exotic and mysterious silhouette is enhanced by the fact the the main *corps-de-logis* is hidden behind a screen wall at the centre of which rises a great archway topped by a stone-carved coat of arms dated 1795.

Inside the courtyard, the main façade lacks the central entrance staircase typical of the Portuguese *quinta.* Instead there are matching flights of steps leading to the corner towers – an arrangement proposed in some eighteenth-century French architectural pattern-books. This plan ensured that the visitor arrived at one end or other of the *enfilade* of internal apartments, rather than at its centre. Curiously, the main part of the house is lower than its adjoining wings, an exact reversal of the usual build-up of architectural emphasis towards the centre.

The typical Minho manor house is raised up over a basement containing cellars where grapes are trod and the wine subsequently matured in great barrels. This is the arrangement at Sezim but it is only apparent from the garden front where the ground level is lower. Here, a long broad verandah with slender iron columns and balustrades runs the length of the house, giving it a distinctly colonial look. The verandah overlooks a formal garden planted as a box parterre, while on the terraces below are shady walks through hooped pergolas on which apple trees have been trained.

Sezim's roofs retain their ancient tiles, now rich with patina, but nowhere is a chimney to be seen. This was a summer house, of which only the kitchen had a chimney. In winter the family took up residence in a palace in Guimarães. Now that Sezim is lived in all year round, the kitchen has become the most frequently used sitting-room.

The principal apartment at Sezim is a surprise and a delight. Double doors open from a vestibule into a salon hung from floor to ceiling with scenic wallpapers. These are the famous 'Views of America' first produced by J. Zuber of Rixheim in Alsace in 1834 and which are often found in early nineteenth-century houses in the United States as well as in Europe. The wallpaper mural to the left of the doors depicts Utah's famous Natural Bridge, a great archway formed of rock; at the right, we see the Niagara Falls. Behind the mirror, one glimpses the spires of Boston. At the other end of the saloon is a view of the Hudson River at West Point. The room has a *Directoire* feel reminiscent of the 1790s; this effect is produced by the curtains, hung from painted rods adorned with pineapples, as well as oval-backed chairs which were made in Portugal after drawings published by the English furniture designer Hepplewhite in 1788.

It takes courage – or disdain, depending how one views it – to hang on a wall one decorative feature over another, the way portraits are sometimes hung over tapestries or mirrors in France. Some of this room's charm stems from the way family portraits are hung over the wallpapers by skewing them to avoid obscuring the main scenes.

After such a dazzling display of brilliantly coloured wallpaper, it is all the more enchanting to find a second and then a third room also treated in this way. The second, smaller salon is hung with more Zuber wallpapers, in this instance portraying Hindustan. These were designed by P.A. Mongin after Daniell's prints of 'Oriental Scenery' and were first produced in 1806. However, as these examples are printed on continuous rolls, they cannot be dated before 1830. The ceiling here, as in the other rooms, is the typical Portuguese trapezoid, with the corners resting on squinches, as in early Ottoman mosques.

The third room in the sequence is the Don Quixote Salon. This has curtains suspended from large arrows adorned with oak wreaths in the centre, again suggesting a date of 1800. Here the scenic wallpapers, though colourful, are decidedly cruder and do not correspond with any of the well-documented French wallpapers of the time. They are

PALÁCIO DA BREJOEIRA. The formal approach to the palatial entrance front. Its straight lines and solid masonry herald the end of the baroque period and the beginning of the Neo-classical architectural style.

probably of Spanish origin. The dado, however, is adorned with a marvellous wallpaper of vaulted Gothic halls, resembling an Italian baroque stage set. This is decidedly French and is, in fact, a frieze illustrating the Don Quixote story, to match the papers above. Beyond is a further small salon hung with canvases painted in imitation of tapestry.

The reference work *Nobres Casas de Portugal* suggests that this house was completed toward the end of the eighteenth century by José Alexandre de Freitas do Amaral Castelo Branco, who died in 1813, and decorated in part by his son Miguel (1797–1856). In the nineteenth century the estate passed through the female line, first to the Melo Sampaio family and then to the Pinto de Mesquita. The present owners, Ambassador Pinto de Mesquita and his wife Maria Francisca, are the first to have made Sezim a family home throughout the year. Sezim, in fact, is a wonderful example of a beautiful, unspoiled country house and estate brought back to life and use without any alterations that might detract from its character.

In 1806, about ten years after the date inscribed on the gateway of the Casa do
Sezim, the construction of the last great country house of the Minho, the Palácio da Brejoeira, was begun. Under almost continuous alteration during the subsequent century – the
private theatre was completed only in the early 1900s – it represents in a very complete
way the history of nineteenth-century country-house architecture in the Minho.

Brejoeira is one of Portugal's grandest houses, with a palatial façade that is
familiar from the labels on the bottles of the estate's distinguished wine. A visit here is all
the more rewarding because this is lonely country, with few villages and great sweeping vistas across low, wooded, rolling hills. An empty straight road leads south from the border
town of Monçao; after about 3 miles, a great park wall on the right announces the estate.
The entrance is heralded by a wrought-iron screen which throws the palace open to
view. The entrance itself comprises a spectacular triple-decked gateway, its stone carved
with baroque voluptuousness.

Inside the gate, the drive divides around a central sunken lawn to arrive at a huge expanse of beautifully raked gravel forming a *cour d'honneur* in front of the entrance façade of the house. The main front has a distinctly Neo-classical feeling, the emphasis on straight lines and solid masonry heralding the end of the baroque. But there are still rococo touches, such as the eared windows in the corner towers and the curved eyebrow pediments above the second-floor windows.

Brejoeira is usually said to date from 1806. This corresponds with the observation of Mrs Dora Wordsworth in her *Journal of a Few Months in Portugal*, published in 1845, that Brejoeira 'was begun about forty years ago'. It was begun by Lúis Pereira Velho de Moscoso, and the work continued until 1834. By this time Lúis Pereira, who was born in 1767, had probably been succeeded by his second son, Simão Pereira, who lived until 1881. Following his death, the estate was sold in about 1901 to Pedro Maria da Fonseca Araújo, president of the Commercial Association of Oporto, who carried out major works of restoration. In 1937 it was sold again, this time to Francisco de Oliveira Pais of Lisbon from whom it was inherited by Maria Herminia da Silva Oliveira who now supervises the estate and the production of its famous wine.

No evidence survives as to who the architect may have been, but the palace has been attributed to Cruz Amarante, the leading designer of this period in the north of Portugal. It is built in the form of an L and has three towers, a plan which suggests that it was originally intended to consist of four equal wings laid out around a courtyard with a tower at each corner. The sheer forcefulness of the design brings to mind two great English baroque houses dating from a century earlier, Castle Howard and Blenheim. All three of these structures include martial features such as trophies of arms and armour; Brejoeira has rain spouts in the form of cannon and, as at Blenheim, the pilasters framing the central pavilion are swept forward in a concave arc.

Great front doors open into a low flagstoned hall at the far side of which is a broad stairway. At the left is the entrance to a perfect little theatre, a rare survival of its kind dating from the early 1900s and complete with tiered seats and a proscenium arch. The painted backdrop is a particularly charming conceit, as it depicts the palace from the front. The tiles on the staircase, attributed to Jorge Pinto, also date from this time. On the first half-landing the staircase opens into a semicircular iron-and-glass conservatory. Today, however, this is not filled with tropical plants but instead holds a bust of the young king who was reigning at the time of the house's completion and serves as a shrine or memorial for him. As the stair continues towards the rear, it branches in two and becomes what is called an imperial stair – an arrangement appropriate to so grand a house. The whole of the second floor consists of an *enfilade* of three large state rooms. To the south is the library, with massive bookcases and a heavy wooden ceiling. This is followed by an audience chamber which contains a canopied throne retaining its original curtains and tassels. Both this room and the next boast massive chandeliers and embossed wallpapers. Overlooking the garden is a state banqueting hall filled with a long table encircled by a splendid array of matching chairs. These state rooms are still regularly put to use: Queen Elizabeth II of England was entertained here on a state visit to Portugal. Although the character of these rooms will seem a little lugubrious to some tastes, no one can leave Brejoeira without feeling privileged to have seen so splendid a house so beautifully maintained.

PALÁCIO DA BREJOEIRA. A rare example of a nineteenth-century private theatre with tiered seat rows and a proscenium arch. The painted backdrop represents a perspective view of the house from the garden.

Below the great banquetting hall lies a spacious box garden of four huge beds filled with great camellias and set around a central tiered fountain encircled by subsidiary fountains representing the Four Elements. A wide avenue extends the view through woodland to the vineyards beyond. Almost invisible nearby is a smaller sunken garden, also planted with camellias, and decorated with a pair of fountains in which the figures of white swans spew water from their beaks.

From the forecourt another straight avenue extends towards a circular, three-storeyed dovecote in the neo-Gothic style. From here, a winding path leads through a wood to a pavilion in the style of a Turkish kiosk. Towards the north end of the same wood the landscape character becomes increasingly fluid, particularly so around an artificial lake. Bold promontories and deep bays prevent the entire surface of the water from being taken in at one glance. Stone bridges and a wooded island are placed so as to conceal the real limits of the water at either end. The deliberately rustic style of the bridges is echoed in a massive grotto of artificial rockwork replete with man-made stalactites beneath its roof. The roof, which is flat, has been converted into a high viewing platform protected by concrete railings which are cast to look like rough natural bark (a popular kind of garden decoration in the late nineteenth century). Bold carriage drives complete the design of this most successful interpretation of the English landscape style of this period in Portugal.

The landscape of Portugal's Minho province is among the most beautiful and unusual in Europe. Because of the verdant abundance of its countryside, its wealth of cheerful towns and the vitality of its folk customs, as well as its many churches, monasteries, bridges and manor houses in delightful baroque and rococo styles, the Minho has always seemed to the people of the less fertile regions of southern Portugal like some distant Arcadia.

Above PALÁCIO DA BREJOEIRA. Rare embossed wallpaper simulating marquetry woodwork, mother-of-pearl inlaid papier mâché furniture and a Chinese *garniture de table* illustrate the inventive and exotic furnishing of the palace's state rooms.

Right PALÁCIO DA BREJOEIRA. The library, with its massive timber bookcases and ceiling in rich, dark tones and its traditional library table, is reminiscent of a room in a turn-of-the-century gentleman's club.

Above PALÁCIO DA BREJOEIRA. The newly
planted semicircular iron-and-glass
conservatory. The bust on the central
pedestal is of the last king of Portugal.

Left PALÁCIO DA BREJOEIRA. A nineteenth-
century tiered fountain occupies the centre
of the clipped camellia garden.

Previous pages PAÇO DE CALHEIROS. The house, with its twin towers, overlooks the wide valley of the Lima river.

PAÇO DE CALHEIROS. The box garden, with its radial pattern around a central pool, forms a foreground to the distant landscape view.

PAÇO DE CALHEIROS. Dark timber ceilings and floors, white-painted walls, granite door and window surrounds, together with English-style Hepplewhite chairs, are typical of the restrained manor-house interiors of the Minho area.

Overleaf SOLAR DE BERTIANDOS. A complex composition in which two separate wings of an eighteenth-century manor house are wrapped around the original sixteenth-century tower-house.

Above PAÇO DA GLÓRIA. Fresh water spills from a stone mask into the swimming pool.

Right PAÇO DA GLÓRIA. Towers and crenellated parapets are an archaic feature of this solid eighteenth-century house with its integrally designed chapel.

Above PAÇO DA GLÓRIA. An hibiscus in front of a decorative window opening, which forms part of the entrance gate to the estate.

Opposite TORRE DOS AZEVEDOS. A sixteenth-century tower was incorporated in the eighteenth-century manor house.

Above CASA DOS BISCAINHOS. The dining-room features scenes painted on canvas which depict romantic subjects. These include tales of despair set by the painter amid picturesque ruins.

Left CASA DOS BISCAINHOS. The principal salon is decorated with Coimbran tiles depicting garden scenes and with a painted and coved ceiling of carved wood.

Left CASA DOS CÓNEGOS. The long
gallery with a remarkable collection
of furniture, objects and paintings.

Above CASA DOS CÓNEGOS. A stone
monster acts as a water spout in the
garden tank.

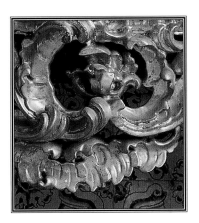

THE
MONDEGO

THE MONDEGO RIVER VALLEY is a vast region of striking contrasts, both naturally and historically. The capital of the coastal region is the ancient university town of Coimbra. In the upland region of the interior known as the Beira Alta, the economy began to forge ahead only after the seventeenth century when the nobility of the area built some large baroque-style manor houses with ornamental chapels and gardens.

The site of the ancient Convento de São Marcos lies downriver from Coimbra. It was established in 1452 on a site given by Queen Isabel to a community of Hieronymite monks. The site had been for centuries the location of a shrine dedicated to São Marcos. The designer of the convent was Gil de Sousa who was also architect of the better-known convent of Penha Longa near Sintra. It was the architect's last commission; he died after its completion and is buried in the chapel.

The chapel's interior is by way of being a pantheon of forgotten heroes and boasts a panoply of sculptural monuments; a Gothic tomb for Fernao Teles de Menezes by the sculptor Diogo Pires the Elder, its canopied stone curtain being held back by figures representing small savages; two Manueline-style tombs, one for Beatriz de Menezes, the convent's founder and the other for a member of the da Silva family. The most important sculptural monument in the chapel is the retable of the main altar. It is the work of Nicolau Chanterène, a great French Renaissance sculptor who worked in Portugal during the early sixteenth century. Sadly, its overall effect is spoiled by some poor nineteenth-century restoration. Also of great interest is the smaller chapel of the Reis Magos which was probably built between 1566 and 1578. With its elegant cupola and lofty dome, it is a fine example of Renaissance architecture. Today the Convento is administered by the University of Coimbra but within its precinct a house is reserved as a residence of the Braganza family.

Another important monastic monument from the Renaissance period survives in Coimbra itself. This is the elaborate covered fountain at the centre of a former cloister garden known as the Jardim da Manga. Heraldic beasts guard the four bridges leading across a pool to the artificial island on which the fountain has been placed. It is a fountain which is important in the context of the development of Portuguese architecture and garden design. It is also important in the wider European context in that its design reflects the influence of the treatise *Hypnerotomachia Poliphilii* written in 1499 by an Italian monk, Fra Francesco Colonna, which had a profound influence on Renaissance garden design.

Downstream from the Convento de São Marcos, in a forest of alder, pine, birch and Spanish chestnut, stands the working estate of Quinta da Foja, which once belonged to the Cruzes order of Coimbra. When the order disbanded in 1834, its forest passed to the state but the convent and its farm passed into private hands. Although the façade of the house is austere, the interior is noted for its elaborate shell-shaped eighteenth-century *azulejos* made in Coimbra. At one time, the *quinta* belonged to the poet João de Lemos but was later bought by the Pinto Basto family who have restored it.

In the town of Condeixa-a-Nova, south of Coimbra and near Conimbriga, one of the major Roman settlements in the Iberian peninsula, is the house known as Casa Soto Maior. Erected in the mid-eighteenth century, it has more the character of a town house than a country house. The austerity of its façade belies the richness of its interior which features much painted and plastered decoration as well as elaborate eighteenth-century Coimbran tilework and inlaid floors. Extensively restored in the 1950s, the house and its chapel contain a fine collection of Portuguese and Indo-Portuguese furniture and objects collected by its owner. The garden, with its box hedging and topiary, also contains a good collection of garden statuary.

The city of Coimbra also contains one of the loveliest botanical gardens in Europe. Because botanic gardens are today conceived mainly as collections of different plants brought together for study, it is rare to find one that has a formal layout. But this was not always the case: in the earliest botanic gardens, such as those in Padua and Pisa in Italy, the collections of plants were accommodated within the strictest of formal layouts.

Early botanical studies in Portugal, as in other European countries, tended to be carried out by members of religious orders. The Jesuits, in particular, combined control of the universities with much missionary activity abroad; their missioners sent back plants from abroad to be studied by their colleagues at home. However, as the religious orders were slow to keep abreast of the new scientific and rationalist thought of the seventeenth century, progressive Portuguese thinkers began to see their hold over the universities as an impediment to the nation's progress. In 1759, the religious orders were expelled from the country by the Marquis of Pombal who then seized the opportunity to modernize universities like Coimbra. There he established a new botanical garden, together with a botanical museum and laboratory, in 1772.

In his efforts to create a new Portugal, Pombal often called on the advice of experts from abroad. He commissioned Colonel William Elsden, an Englishman, to make a plan for the new garden and Domenico Vandelli and Giulio Mazziatti, both Italian, to serve respectively as its first director and planting assistant. On a steep slope below the university, an

area of approximately two acres was levelled, terraced and divided into beds narrow enough to allow close observation of the plants. The area was enclosed within high walls and entered by large ornamental gates. Known as the Coimbra, Valley and Queen Maria gates respectively, they were completed between 1791 and 1794 and still grace the garden today.

The garden became fully established between 1791 and 1811 under its distinguished director Dr Félix de Avelar Brotero who was concurrently director of the Royal Botanic Gardens at Ajuda. By 1807 over 4,000 taxa were being cultivated, and a corner for the specialized study of tropical plants had been established. Laura Junot, wife of the French Ambassador to Portugal (1808–11), recorded that the garden compared favourably with the Jardin des Plantes in Paris and recommended it as an ideal place in which to study 'the curious and beautiful flora of Portugal'.

The garden gradually became the most important institution of its kind in the country. Major architectural works were undertaken – the Stairs of Honour (1814–21), the Main Gate (1842) and the Great Glasshouse (1856). The latter remained the most substantial structure of its kind in Portugal until the completion of the Estufa Quente in Lisbon in 1975. By 1862, the garden had reached its present size of 50 acres. Dr Júlio Henriques, the greatest of the garden's directors, arrived in 1873. His first task was the restoration of the garden's museum. This was followed by the restoration of the garden's herbarium, known as the Willdenow Herbarium, one of its greatest treasures.

The late nineteenth century was a period of rapid development in botanic gardens all over the world and of the interchange of both knowledge and plants. Coimbra benefited from its director's friendship with Baron von Mueller, the famous director of the Melbourne Botanic Gardens in Australia. Von Mueller not only wrote the first substantial account of many of Australia's trees and shrubs but exported seed from them to other parts of the world. In this way many members of the eucalyptus and acacia families reached Portugal for the first time. From Melbourne came much of Coimbra's beautiful collection of eucalyptus and its enormous Moreton Bay fig, *Ficus macrophylla.*

Because interest in ornamental gardening burgeoned during the nineteenth century, botanic gardens were forced to expand their collections of useful plants to include those of a purely ornamental nature, and to allow entry to the public on a regular basis. At the Jardim Botanico, a shady linden avenue was planted to make a promenade, the original quadrangle was enhanced with a fountain, seats were built, decorative box hedging planted, and commemorative busts of the garden's distinguished botanists were erected – a charming feature of many Portuguese botanic gardens.

Along the upper reaches of the Mondego river, at the heart of the famous Dão wine region, lie the towns of Viseu and Mangualde around which are located some of the most elegant and characteristic manor houses of Portugal.

CASA ANADIA

The main front of the Casa Anadia stands right on the road leading into the little town of Mangualde. It is not especially big or imposing, but the public road takes a deferential twist to the left, skirting the walls by a few yards. The house has two storeys, the taller upper windows indicating that the main rooms are on the upper floor. The elaborately carved stone entrance portal has a massive balcony, and there is a richly treated window on the upper floor. It has the little ears and sections of rippling pediment that so appealed to Portuguese masons of the baroque period. The other windows on either side have an unusual detail: carved stone 'aprons' hanging beneath the sills. Interestingly the windows here are casements of the French type, rather than sashes often found in Portugal, but above these the builders have contrived upper windows with highly unusual glazing bars.

By contrast, the inner courtyard façade has a deep set arcade on two storeys, with two arches below and four above. The lower arcade is approached by a delightful horseshoe-shaped stairway that ascends in two curving flights around an open centre. The upper loggia is elaborately treated within; the windows have characteristic baroque tweaked pediments; above them is an elaborately painted ceiling. The walls are panelled with tiles cut to form a crest of ornamental finials.

The building and decoration of the palace were evidently carried out over the best part of a century, probably involving some four generations of the family. The main structure appears to have been built by Miguel Pais do Amaral and probably dates from the 1730s or 1740s. His son, also called Miguel Pais do Amaral, married Dona Joaquina Teodora de Sã e Menezes in 1749. They were probably responsible for the rococo tiles

inside. Their son, Simão Pais, was succeeded by his eldest son, also called Miguel Pais. The property then passed to his brother, Manuel de Sã Pais do Amaral, who in 1821 married the Condessa de Anadia who brought the Anadia title into the family.

As usual in Portugal, it is the tiles which help date the interiors. The hall is relatively plain, but an elaborate archway opens up into an immensely grand staircase. This is an imperial staircase, with one flight branching into two. The massive stone handrail is carved on solid walls, allowing the maximum space for tiled decoration. On the flanks of the lower flight are large hunting scenes, with an architectural base designed to look like a handrail.

The hunting scenes continue on the half-landing, with the tile-pictures breaking the bounds of their frames. This feature, as well as the urns and scrolls cut out in silhouette, is a common baroque conceit. It is carried to extremes on the upper-floor landing where the centre of each tile panel is swept up in an extravagant burst of scrollwork ornament. Originally tilework borders such as these rose no higher than a chair-rail aligned on the tops of the back of the rooms' chairs. But in Portugal during the baroque period these borders rose with ever-increasing extravagance to head and shoulder height on the wall.

For all the explosion of curves and curls, the tilework detail on the staircase and in the main saloon is not yet rococo; this suggests a date in the 1730s and 1740s. The main

CASA ANADIA. In early spring, the lace-like tracery of the courtyard plane tree is repeated in shadow on the sandy floor.

Below CASA ANADIA. The courtyard's elegant horseshoe-shaped stairs rise to the entrance loggia. The loggia above enjoys distant views of the Serra de Marão mountains.

Right CASA ANADIA. The old kitchen is no less beautifully maintained than the rest of the house. Painted blue and white, its highly polished copper cooking utensils reflect the light as if they were mirrors.

CASA ANADIA. A hunter and his hound chasing a hare, a stag and a partridge into the sea, together with fish flying improbably through the air, are depicted in this fantastical tile-picture.

saloon also has a very fine set of splat-back armchairs and a settee, very much in the manner of early eighteenth-century chairs in England, though the gilding adds a still more exuberant note. In the music room, the tiles are rococo with characteristic shell-work and the strong yellow colour which was added to the traditional blue and white colours at this time – all suggesting a date in the 1780s.

The library, by contrast, is strongly Neo-classical with simple and severely rectangular built-in bookcases. It must date from twenty to thirty years later. Intriguingly, it has a vaulted ceiling, very much in the manner of the English architect Sir John Soane whose house (now a museum) in Lincoln's Inn Fields in London is full of rooms with cross-vaulted ceilings like this. The decoration of the room is simple, with a characteristic repeating border. The old kitchen of the house is no less beautifully maintained than the rest of the estate. It is painted in blue and white, with highly polished brass cooking utensils reflecting the light as if they were mirrors.

During the early eighteenth century in France, and later in England, the idea arose that a garden need not be confined to the area around a house and also that it need not be screened off from the farmland around. Ornamental gardening could be, it was decided, used to beautify every part of an estate – a decision that created what came to be known as a *ferme ornée* or, in English, an ornamental farm. In practice this implied not only the planting of groves of trees but also the laying out of pleasant walks through the fields. Pastures and cornfields previously regarded as mere productive units were now seen as pleasant features to look at and enjoy. Grass walks were mown around cornfields. Gravel walks, sometimes lined with flowering shrubs, were laid out around pastures. At intervals along the walks a seat, a summer-house or even a fountain would be placed. Although Portugal was only lightly touched by this gardening fashion, the garden at Anadia provides an enchanting example. From behind the house, a long box-hedged walk stretches out among the fields, shaded here and there by mixed groves of evergreen oaks, chestnuts, planes and pines. At one point along its length, a cross-walk leads to a monumental wall-fountain painted pink and yellow ochre and surrounded by seats. At a further point along its length, another cross-walk leads to a topiary garden with a fountain and pool unexpectedly located among the farm's fields. From here, further walks continue out into the estate, providing charming views of vineyards, apple orchards, cornfields, woodland and pasture. Casa Anadia has a beguiling example of the *ferme ornée* which is a living testimonial to the words of the poet Horace:

> He that the beautiful and useful blends
> Simplicity with greatness, gains all ends.

Several miles beyond Mangualde near the town of Penalva do Castelo is the Casa de Ínsua, a country house that is truly seigneurial, not merely a retreat or hunting lodge. It is very much the hub of an estate, complete with *cour d'honneur*, dependencies, well-tended formal gardens, woodland walks and many ornamental farm buildings. One catches the first glimpse of Insua across its vineyards. Even on a clear day there is a slight sense of mystery, for it is difficult to pick out the villa's silhouette against the dark mass of trees behind it; moreover, the pointed windows and low, pyramidal roofs give it an exotic touch suggestive of Portugal's far-flung former colonies.

A few dozen yards further on, a powerful trio of gates with stone piers announces the estate. Its style – with models of Renaissance ships and a Latin inscription announcing 'joyfully we salute our guests' – suggests a date of 1900. But today this drive is closed and the road skirts around beneath a topiary garden to the little village church. Here a mighty gate stands immediately beside the house and leads into a beautiful, secluded courtyard shaded by noble plane trees and a huge eucalyptus.

The main part of the house is on the right. Low windows at the ground level are sturdily protected by a grid of iron bars; at one place, however, a former doorway has been blocked and bears the characteristic bulbous grill found all over Iberia. The main entrance, with a delightful rippling pediment, rises to the height of the second-level windows, which have bold diamond lattices on either side. Further along are characteristic Portuguese sashes. At the bottom corners of the upper windows, little feet rest on neatly carved scrolls that look like rolls of parchment tied with string. On either side of the main entrance is a series of small cannon variously dated from 1776 to 1797.

At the end of the courtyard is the chapel, while on the left is a lower range of outbuildings, with an archway leading through to the farmyard and winery beyond. In the centre of the courtyard is a fountain at which oxen still drink. Insua's main façade, overlooking the garden, has taller end-pavilions treated like towers with pointed battlements pierced by *fleurs-de-lis*. Crenellations like these were a feature of Portuguese keeps during the late Middle Ages and Renaissance; they must have been introduced here to give the house an appearance of antiquity. They are equipped with stone water spouts carved like the barrels of cannon. Both end-pavilions are inset with arcaded loggias. The windows above have pretty ironwork balconies reminiscent of the engraved designs for *maisons de plaisance* by French eighteenth-century architects like Blondel or Briseux.

Ínsua was built for Luís de Albuquerque (1739–97). The Portuguese Albuquerques are distinct from the Spanish grandees of the same name, forming a separate line; Luís was a descendant of Afonso de Albuquerque, a great figure in sixteenth-century Portuguese India. Luis was appointed governor of the important province of Matto Grosso in northern Brazil and entrusted with the immense task of defining its frontier with the Spanish territories beyond. Ínsua's date is uncertain, but is probably not earlier than 1760 when Luis was but twenty-one. More likely, the house dates from the 1770s or 1780s.

Insua's dates are certainly too late for Nasoni, the great Tuscan architect working in Oporto, to have been its architect. It was more likely built by one of his first-rate disciples. The most probable candidate is José Francisco de Paiva (1744–1824). Paiva's work is the subject of an excellent catalogue published in Lisbon in 1973; from his drawings and notes it is evident that he made extensive use of English and French pattern books. The rococo wrought-iron balconies on his houses in Oporto are clearly influenced by Briseux's plates and strongly resemble the balconies of Ínsua. Another parallel can be drawn with the church of the Convent of S. Bento de Avé-Maria in Oporto, also attributed to Paiva, and where the rippling pediments are similar to those at Insua.

Inside the house, the stone hall is hung with trophies – mainly spears and blow-pipes – and is dominated by massive stone stairs with solid sides coiled like springs in the corners to give a strongly baroque effect. In the house is a well-preserved set of French scenic wallpapers manufactured by J. Zuber of Rixheim whose papers are also found at the Casa de Sezim in the Minho. This set dates from 1827 and the artist responsible was J.M.Gué, a pupil of David.

The 100-acre park of Insua is ringed with upwards of 400 Italian cypresses planted in 1910. Many of them are now 75–100 feet tall and give the landscape an unexpectedly Tuscan flavour. Immediately beneath the garden front of the house is a long stone-edged canal that provides a beautiful reflection of the façade – another oriental touch. The box garden is even longer than the house, part of it in a *fleur-de-lis* pattern to commemorate the marriage of the present Duke's sister. Here, as elsewhere in Portugal, the pattern of the box parterre is often discreetly adapted to commemorate an important event in the life of the family or estate. In another corner of Insua's garden, the long service of a head gardener is remembered in a design in box made up of his initials plus a crossed shovel and rake.

CASA DA ÍNSUA. This wall-fountain is characterized by a severity in design and austerity of tile colour, an effect underlined by its stone-carved suits of armour.

In the centre of the box parterre is a circular outdoor 'room' enclosed by high walls of clipped camellias. Here, in a stone-edged pool grows a group of nelumbos, large-leaved cousins of the more familiar lotus flower of India. On either side of the 'room' are gigantic clipped camellia 'umbrellas' and a Yulan magnolia dated 1842. The date shows this to be one of the earliest magnolias grown in Portugal. Beyond the main section, another box garden is laid out in the shape of a giant fan. Shasta daisies, roses, cannas and salvias now fill the box patterns with strong accents of colour which are echoed on the white walls of the house by great sprays of bougainvillea, Cape honeysuckle and morning glory.

A 300-yard-long tunnel of high box trees provides a shady promenade. Said to have been planted in 1775, it has many counterparts in other Portuguese gardens but it was gradually found to be too confined in shape and space for walking. So a woodland garden was created in the trees behind the house in the late nineteenth century. A multiplicity of axial walks, each bearing an individual name such as Rua Helena, was projected under a canopy of native oak and pine, eucalyptus, Californian redwood and cedar of Goa. One walk leads to a pond with an island reached by a little hump-backed bridge; another features a menagerie while yet another leads to a religious shrine with a terracotta altarpiece of the Virgin and Child signed by L. Battistini (1900). One of the many fountains which lighten the wood is of particular interest in that its pool is inset with stone-edged flower-beds – a 1,500-year-old tradition in Portugal; similar stone-edged beds grace garden pools in the villas of the Roman settlement of Conimbriga not far away. It is thought that many of these picturesque features were designed by Nicola Bigaglia, an inventive architect who was employed on the estate about 1895. In any case, these many and unique attractions ensure Insua's position as the most comprehensively designed of all the gardens in the province of Beira Alta.

West of Insua and near the town of Viseu is the third of the trinity of fine houses and gardens in this area, the Casa de Santar. The house's main attraction is its double-tiered roof, each tier having an exotic upward eaves-tilt in the style known as Pombaline after the great Marquess of Pombal. Also contributing to the elegance of its roofline are the chimneys, each of which is designed to look like a dovecote in miniature. Although the garden's outline follows the irregular line of the public road and the alignment of its central axis changes halfway through its sequence of three terraces, all else is conventional. On each terrace, waist-high box hedges enclose a complex pattern of lower box hedges and flower-beds filled with floribunda roses in muted colour schemes. Stone balustrades and clipped box pyramids provide visual accents.

Although the garden dates from the eighteenth century, it was extensively restored at the beginning of this century. During the restoration, the 1790 wall-fountain was also rebuilt. Its centre is surmounted by a coat of arms beneath which a grotesque mask spews water into a stone trough. The tile-pictures on the wall on either side depict equestrian figures like those above the tank at Palacio de Fronteira. However, they are the work of José Maria Pereira Cão, carried out at the beginning of this century. The faces of the horsemen are portraits of family members of that time. The unusual configuration of the ground and the shift in alignment of the garden's main axis save this conventional design from dullness, as does the high quality of the garden's maintenance.

The eighteenth-century garden of Castelo Branco, although not located in the Mondego valley, lies in a remote but prosperous town south-east of Viseu near the Spanish border. Set as it is in the mountains of Estrela, its inland climate can be harsh; winters are often cold and summers unbearably dry and hot. In 1598 the local Bishop of Guarda built an episcopal palace in the town and laid out a garden around it. However, in 1725 one of his successors remodelled both palace and garden and it is his work we appreciate today.

From the windows of the palace, now a museum, it is possible to look out over an elaborate box parterre towards an amphitheatre of terraces and staircases which encloses the garden on two sides. The parterre comprises 24 small box-edged beds in all, the middle eight being grouped around a fountain basin of unusually delicate floral shape. The complicated division and sub-division of large box gardens to form a multiplicity of small beds is characteristic of the Portuguese garden. Here the already crowded effect is increased by the addition of many granite figures.

On the first terrace opposite the palace is a raised water tank known as the Crown Pond on account of the three granite crowns raised high above the water on granite shafts. The terrace above it holds another tank of unusual trapezoidal shape in which is arranged a set of stone-edged flower-beds in an arabesque pattern. Such flower islets are common in Portuguese gardens of every age but none has the fluidity of design shown here. Further terraces have ornamental gateways and orange groves.

CASA DA ÍNSUA. The long garden façade, with its rococo window details, is reflected in the waters of the adjoining tank.

CASA DA ÍNSUA. The box garden seen from a first-floor balcony. The box garden has been romanticized by the rounded clipping of the pattern's corners. Clipped camellia 'umbrellas' are typical of gardens in northern Portugal.

The garden is remarkable for its unique collection of granite garden statuary, all of which appears to have been made in the same provincial, if not local, school of sculpture. All of the figures are slightly smaller than life size. Stylized in conception and execution, perhaps on account of the difficulty of carving hard granite, they have struck some, like the English writer Sacheverell Sitwell, as 'wooden in effect'. None the less they possess an archaic charm because they are conceived in thematic groups. Figures of the Twelve Apostles and of the Four Evangelists – appropriate figures for an episcopal garden – deck the balustrades of one terrace, the Kings of Portugal another. In an ironic twist, those kings who were forced to suffer Spanish domination are depicted as smaller than the others. Elsewhere are similar figures depicting the Signs of the Zodiac, the Four Seasons, the Four Cardinal Virtues, the Four Points of the Compass and the Four States of the Soul. By 1910 the garden had fallen into severe disrepair. Five years later, however, it underwent extensive restoration. It still surprises the visitor with an intricacy of detail and design that is unexpected in a provincial town.

The collection of trees at Ínsua was mentioned earlier. However, the most extraordinary collection of trees in the region grows not far away at Buçaco. As early as the sixth century this natural forest of oak, pine, laurestinus and phillyrea was a place of peace and seclusion for hermits and holy men. In 1622, to protect their solitary and contemplative way of life, Pope Gregory XV issued a papal edict forbidding women to enter the forest's precincts. In 1628, Carmelite friars set up a monastery at its centre, building a high wall around 260 acres. In 1643, Pope Urban VII issued an edict forbidding, under pain of excommunication, the felling of any forest trees, thus ensuring their preservation. The substance of the papal edict was carved in stone over the Coimbra Gate and can still be read today.

The Carmelites' careful husbandry of the forest resulted in the introduction at Buçaco of what is thought to be the first European colony of cedar of Goa, *Cupressus lusitanica*, which in spite of its name is a native of Mexico. The tree is thought to have been introduced by missioners in 1653. The largest specimen in the forest today carries a brass plate indicating an earlier planting date of 1644, but this has not been authenticated. By 1906, the number of cedars, according to Veitch's *Manual on Conifers* had increased to 'upwards of five thousand seven hundred including one of colossal growth which is nearly one hundred feet high with a girth of twelve feet'. Occasionally, and then only for important visitors, the law prohibiting the entrance of women into the forest was relaxed. Catarina of Braganza was granted the privilege of a visit on her return to Portugal after the death of her husband, Charles II of England. The gate known as the Queen's Gate was erected in her honour and was subsequently used by all distinguished female visitors.

In the late seventeenth century, the forest came under the protection of João de Melo, the Count-Bishop of Coimbra. He laid out the Via Sacra, a holy way rising from the monastery to the highest point in the forest, called the Cruz Alta because of the great stone crucifix that had been erected there. The ascent is marked by a series of baroque chapels, each sheltering a life-like scene, executed in terracotta of a stage in Christ's Passion.

In 1722, a Carmelite chronicler praised the forest's luxuriant undergrowth of evergreen shrubs – privet, Portugal laurel, laurstinus and phillyrea – and sweet-smelling herbs such as honeysuckle, sweet betony and royal clover. The forest's tranquillity was shattered in 1810 when the combined Portuguese and English armies under the command of the Duke of Wellington defeated there a division of Napoleon's army under the command of General Massena.

In 1834 during one of the waves of anti-clericalism that swept Portugal, the Carmelites were obliged to leave Buçaco and with their departure its history as a primarily sacred place came to an end. After a brief period in private ownership, the forest became state property in 1859. The new director, Dom Rodrigo de Morais Soares, developed the lands immediately around the former monastery as an arboretum of rare trees. The hospitality of the climate encouraged a cosmopolitan collection of species. For example, a bunya-bunya pine from Australia grows near a European olive tree, a Himalayan deodar rises next to a specimen of North American white ash and a crepe myrtle from India. Nearby the branches of a Californian Monterey pine mingle with those of Morocco's Atlas cedar, and a camphor tree from Japan shares a site with an Australian black wattle.

In 1881, a valley below the monastery was landscaped. A spring of limpid water, known as the Cold Spring or Fonte Fria, was directed down a flight of 144 steps to make a formal cascade flowing into a shady pool bordered by hydrangeas and magnolias. Further down the valley, the stream flows into a large artificial lake, its shadowy surface reflecting the silhouettes of many exotic trees. Included are the aromatic *Umbellularia californica*, a Douglas fir – reputedly among the largest in Europe – and a specimen of California's Santa Lucia fir, *Abies bracteata,* thought by many to be the most ornamental of the fir family. The large shining leaves of *Firmiana simplex* stand out in this arboreal tapestry through which the stream descends further into the Valley of the Ferns, which gets its name from the Australasian tree ferns which cover its sides.

In 1888, a royal palace was projected adjoining the former monastery. Designed by Luigi Mannini, the Italian stage-designer (see Quinta da Regaleira) in the late Portuguese Gothic style known as Manueline, it was still under construction at the time of King Carlos's assassination in 1908. Following the dethroning of his son, Manuel II, and the subsequent proclamation of the Portuguese Republic in 1910, the building, the last major country house to be built in central Portugal, was converted into the luxurious hotel which it remains today.

Above CASA ANADIA. An explosion of decorative detail characterizes these tile-pictures which depict mythological themes such as that of Apollo and his lyre. The inlaid table is seventeenth-century Venetian.

Opposite CASA ANADIA. The state rooms boast elaborate tiled dados. Their manufacture is attributed to the Rato factory in Lisbon. Gilded details give to the splat-back settee a note of exuberance.

Right CASA ANADIA. A comic, moral fable in which a donkey and his master change places is the subject of this humourous tile.

Above CASA ANADIA. The delicate
decoration of the Neo-classical suite
of rooms on the ground floor includes
monochrome rosaille medallions of
Chinese inspiration.

Right CASA ANADIA. The dining-room, with
its vaulted ceiling in the manner of Sir John
Soane, is also part of this suite of rooms.
Their size and intimacy make them ideal for
contemporary family life.

Above CASA ANADIA. The intimate Neo-classical suite of rooms on the ground floor includes a library with fitted bookcases of a delicate and restrained design.

Right CASA ANADIA. An upright eighteenth-century secretaire of 'architectural' design filled with compartments. secret and otherwise.

Above CASA ANADIA. A lace-bonnetted nineteenth-century ancestress of the Anadia family.

Opposite CASA ANADIA. Rococo asymmetry in design characterizes this gilded console table and mirror as well as the porcelain basket on the table.

Left CASA ANADIA. An Italian marble-inlaid table top features a view of a hunter and his quarry. The picture's decorative surround contains accurate depictions of such garden flowers as ranunculus and tulips.

JARDIM BOTÁNICO, COIMBRA. The steep-sided valley in which the garden is sited allows dramatic, panoramic views from the upper terraces.

BIBLIOGRAPHY

AFONSO, SIMONETTA LUZ, *O Palácio de Queluz*, Lisbon, 1986

AFONSO, SIMONETTA LUZ and DELAFORCE, ANGELA, *Palace of Queluz – The Gardens*, Lisbon, 1989

ALEXANDER, BOYD, *The Journal of William Beckford in Portugal and Spain 1787-1788*, London, 1954

ARAÚJO, ILÍDIO ALVES DE, *Arte Paisagista e Arte dos Jardins em Portugal*, Lisbon, 1962

AZEREDO, FRANCISCO DE, *Casa Senhoriais Portuguesas*, Barcelos, 1986

AZEVEDO, CARLOS DE, *Solares Portugueses*, Lisbon, 1969.

BINNEY, MARCUS, 'Casa da Ínsua', *Country Life*, London, 31 May 1983

—, 'Quinta da Regaleira', *Country Life*, London, 16 June 1983

—, *Country Manors of Portugal*, Lisbon, New York and Woodbridge, 1987

BOWE, PATRICK, *Gardens of Portugal*, New York, Lisbon and London, 1989

—, *Parcs et Jardins des plus belles demeures de Portugal*, Paris, 1990

CARDOSO, PEDRO HOMEM and CARITA, HÉLDER, *Da Grandeza dos Jardins em Portugal*, Lisbon, 1987

—, *Portuguese Gardens*, Woodbridge, 1990

COSTA, FRANCISCO, *História da Quinta e Palácio de Monserrate, Sintra*, n.d.

GUERRA, LUIS FIGUEIREDO DA, 'Torres Solarengos do Alto Minho', *O Instituto*, vol. 72, no.4, Coimbra, 1925

HAUPT, ALBRECHT, *A Arquitectura do Renascimento em Portugal*, Lisbon, 1986

JUNOT, LAURA, *Souvenirs d'une Ambassade et d'un Séjour en Espagne et au Portugal*, Paris, 1837

LARA, LUÍS FILIPE DE ALBUQUERQUE DE SOUSA, *Parque do Monteiro-Mor*, Lisbon, 1978

LINO, RAÚL, 'O Estilo na Casa Portuguesa do século XVII', *Revista Municipal*, no. 16, Lisbon, 1943

MARKL, DAGOBERTO, 'O Renascimento', *História da Arte em Portugal*, Lisbon, 1986

MECO, JOSÉ, Catálogo da exposição 'Azulejos de Lisboa', Lisbon, 1984

NICHOLS, ROSE STANDISH, *Spanish and Portuguese Gardens*, Boston, 1924

PAGE, RUSSELL, 'Some Portuguese Gardens', *Landscape and Garden*, London, 1935

PEREIRA, ARTUR D., *Sintra and its Farm Manors*, Sintra, 1983

PEREIRA, JOSÉ FERNANDES, *Arquitectura barocca em Portugal*, Lisbon, 1986

RASTEIRO, JOAQUIM, *Quinta e Palácio da Bacalhoa em Azeitão*, Lisbon, 1895–8

SANTOS, REYNALDO DOS, *O Azulejo em Portugal*, Lisbon, 1957

SIMÕES, J.M. DOS SANTOS, *Azulejaria em Portugal nos séculos xv e xvi*, Lisbon, 1969

—, *Azulejaria em Portugal no século xvii*, Lisbon, 1971

SITWELL, SACHEVERELL, *Portugal and Madeira*, London, 1946

SMITH, ROBERT, *The Art of Portugal, 1500-1800*, London, 1968

STOOP, ANNE DE, *Quintas e Palácios nos Arredores de Lisboa*, Porto, 1986

VITERBO, FRANCISCO MARQUES DE SOUSA, *A Jardinagem em Portugal*, 2 vols., Coimbra, 1906 and 1909

WATSON, WALTER CRUM, *Portuguese Architecture*, London, 1909

—, *Guia de Portugal*, 3 vols., Lisbon, 1983–4

INDEX